JUDITH VON HALLE, born in Berlin in 1972, attended school in Germany and the USA and subsequently studied architecture, graduating in 1998. She first encountered anthroposophy in 1997, and began working as a member of staff at Rudolf Steiner House in Berlin, where she also lectured from 2001. In addition she had her own architectural practice. In 2004 she received the stigmata, which transformed her life. Her first book was published in German in 2005, and she now works principally as a lecturer and author. She lives in Berlin with her husband.

PETER TRADOWSKY, born in Berlin in 1934, has worked as an upper school teacher. Since 1972 he has been the director of the Anthroposophisch-Pädagogisches Seminar. He is the founder of Rudolf Steiner Haus in Berlin and a key staff member of the Arbeitszentrum. He is a frequent lecturer and the author of many books.

D1561586

By the same author:

The Lord's Prayer, The Living Word of God

AND IF HE HAS NOT BEEN RAISED . . .

The Stations of Christ's Path to Spirit Man

JUDITH VON HALLE

With contributions from Peter Tradowsky

TEMPLE LODGE

Translated from German by Brian Strevens

Temple Lodge Publishing
Hillside House, The Square
Forest Row, RH18 5ES

www.templelodge.com

Published by Temple Lodge 2007

Originally published in German under the title *'Und wäre Er nicht auferstanden . . .', Die Christus-Stationen auf dem Weg zum geistigen Menschen* by Verlag am Goetheanum, Dornach, in 2005

Quotations from the Bible have been taken from the Oxford University Revised Version, 1898

A catalogue record for this book is available from the British Library

ISBN 978 1902636 88 7

Cover by Andrew Morgan Design featuring *Damnation and Salvation* by Lucas Cranach the Elder
Typeset by DP Photosetting, Neath, West Glamorgan
Printed and bound by Cromwell Press Limited, Trowbridge, Wiltshire

And if Christ has not been raised,
our preaching is useless
and so is your faith.

Paul, 1 Corinthians 15:14

A note on the cover

The front cover illustration features a detail from the 1529 painting *Damnation and Salvation* by Lucas Cranach the Elder, in the Schlossmuseum Gotha.

It is an allegorical painting referring to the evolution of mankind and the Earth before and after the Christ event. The painting is divided into two halves by a tree (left picture edge). The detail shown is the side illustrating 'Salvation'. Christ, the 'new Adam' who (according to Paul in Corinthians 15:45–49 and Romans 5:14), by His Sacrifice on the Cross, redeems the first, the fallen Adam, who is raising his hands in a gesture of adoration. The living blood of the Redeemer, which is spurting out of the side wound, penetrates first the head of His herald, John the Baptist—a clear reference to his beheading—before finally reaching Adam.

Christ's descent into Hell is represented by the symbol of the Lamb conquering Lucifer and Ahriman—serpent and death. In the background, above the opened rock tomb, is the Resurrection form of the Lord within the sun circle.

The pouring out of the spirit of Whitsun can be recognized in the fiery angel descending from the cosmic sun.

In the left background is a splendid city, the 'New Jerusalem' (Apocalypse).

Contents

Foreword

The seven lectures brought together in the present book were held by Judith von Halle and Peter Tradowsky in Rudolf Steiner Haus, Berlin, between Michaelmas 2004 and Whitsun 2005.

The specific reason for the first lectures was the stigmatization of Judith von Halle occurring at Passiontide 2004. For various reasons, which will be gone into in the Introduction which follows, the decision was made to present what had happened at first to a small circle of members of the Anthroposophical Society in Berlin. The first two lectures therefore are given over essentially to this occurrence and the phenomena connected with it. There are basically two prevailing tendencies when a judgement is made in relation to the phenomenon of stigmatization. The facts are either simply denied or described as a sheer miracle. Here the attempt will be made on the basis of the spiritual-scientific knowledge of Rudolf Steiner to come at least to a preliminary understanding of the inexhaustible depths of this phenomenon and its decisive influence on the course of destiny.

In the five lectures which follow, the events of the life of Christ—the turning-point in world history—experienced as a consequence of the stigmatization are described and explored by means of spiritual-scientific knowledge. Tied to this is the hope, and this is also an important reason for publication in book form, that these lectures may stimulate the reader to reflect patiently and repeatedly upon the Mystery of Golgotha and to enter into an ever more close relationship to the Christ impulse.

These lectures were not recorded or taken down in writing, but were written down later in a form which tries to retain the spontaneity of the spoken word.

Peter Tradowsky
Midsummer 2005

Introduction

As the preliminary remarks of Peter Tradowsky indicate the following lectures were open only to members of the Anthroposophical Society, since it is my conviction that my destiny is linked directly to the Anthroposophical Society. Now the question can be asked why then are the contents of these lectures being published in a book intended for a wider readership than this circle of people—perhaps the lecturer has not remained true to her convictions. This question is justified. The answer is not easy to give and it was a long, inner journey before coming to the decision to publish. The circle of people to whom I wish to open myself in this way I still see as being essentially within the Anthroposophical Society, since its members have possibilities for dealing with the phenomenon in itself described here, and the esoteric information, that are not available to people unfamiliar with the spiritual science of Rudolf Steiner. The lectures presume a basic knowledge of Anthroposophy and therefore contain terms formed and used by Rudolf Steiner, which someone new to Anthroposophy might not be familiar with. This is not intended in any way to deny those who do not belong to the Anthroposophical Society any awareness of the spiritual world nor any understanding for the contents of the lectures. However it has to be taken into account that the manner in which the lectures, reproduced here in written form, were held was aimed at an audience having some previous knowledge.

A few of the reasons which led to the decision to publish the lectures are presented here briefly.

For one thing many people who had heard or would have liked to have heard the lectures approached me with the request for a transcript. In addition, over time another aspect emerged: speculation and rumour-mongering, due primarily to inadequate awareness, arose as the news of my fate spread through the anthroposophical movement and resulted to some extent in my person being identified with the occurrence of the stigmatization. The present publication is intended to give those people who could not hear the lectures the possibility of also being able to judge for themselves.

But the hope I have above all for this book is that consideration may be given to that which I place at the heart of my efforts: to achieve through psychic and spiritual contemplation of the most decisive and fateful event in the development of mankind a living and truthful relationship to the contemporary Christ. This alone is capable of being each single individual's most precious treasure and will be the quiet source of all selfless love and sympathy.

This Introduction will therefore refer to a few facts which I did not want to mention when giving the lectures since—when conveyed personally—they can all too easily be misunderstood or inadvertently given too much prominence. Certain developments which I would like to describe briefly in the following now compel me, however, contrary to my original intentions, to state these facts openly and unambiguously.

In the initial planning for the lectures only the first three were envisaged. After several months of hiding the stigmatization as well as a period of inner conflict and struggle over how to deal with the events in a dignified way, the decision was taken to hold an internal presentation within the membership of the Berlin Arbeitszentrum. The first lecture was intended to explain the phenomenon of stigmatization as well as to include an initial approach to a spiritual scientific understanding on the basis of Rudolf Steiner's lecture cycle *From Jesus to Christ* (GA 131).★ The second lecture was intended to explore the causes of the phenomenon from an understanding of the human being. The first two lectures were in fact given along these lines. The third lecture was intended to examine the psychic and spiritual perception directly tied to the appearance of the stigmatization.

But a second element was meant to be discernible in this lecture. Underlying the details given was another kind of psychic and spiritual experience than the direct perception of the events of the life of Christ. This other kind of spiritual experience encompasses potentially every area imaginable. It is not connected to the phenomenon of the stigmatization, but was already present *before* it. It can be described as a psychic and spiritual awareness beyond the threshold to the spiritual

---

★ See p. 177 for details of this and other works by Rudolf Steiner referred to throughout.

world. During the lectures I avoided speaking in any way whatsoever about the ability to perceive in this way as I assumed that the audience would be perfectly able to distinguish these differing ways of communicating historical facts on the one hand, and purely spiritual facts on the other hand. The lectures which followed and which no longer addressed the phenomenon of the stigmatization should have spoken for themselves through their content without any specific reference to the above mentioned manner of psychic and spiritual vision having to be made.

There are two reasons though why I have now decided to say something about this spiritual awareness. The one reason is that—as I heard later—some individuals apparently had difficulties clearly determining which statements originated from Rudolf Steiner and which ones from me. The confusion increased as these individuals sought vainly in Rudolf Steiner's Complete Works for details about the subjects dealt with. The possibility of such confusion was not present in my mind since I had mentioned constantly and clearly when I was quoting an insight from Rudolf Steiner. Finally my attention was drawn to the fact that often lectures held in the Anthroposophical Society investigate primarily the results of Rudolf Steiner's spiritual research—interwoven with the insights of the lecturer with regard to the corresponding subject investigated by Rudolf Steiner.

I have intentionally devised the five lectures which constitute the central content of this book in such a way that descriptions are mainly given which are not to be found in Rudolf Steiner's lectures. The necessity demanded by Rudolf Steiner of speaking openly about truths one has lived through, the spiritual knowledge connected with them, and of describing them as well as possible was for me also a necessity. In order to avoid any misunderstandings I would like to stress that all my descriptions are only possible because I have, just like every other member of the Anthroposophical Society, Rudolf Steiner's Anthroposophy as a basis for all spiritual research. Not one single word in the lectures which attempts to show the spiritual context of the Mystery of Golgotha and its background could be spoken without the spiritual science inaugurated by Rudolf Steiner. Each individual at present incarnated on the Earth who feels himself truly connected to Anthroposophy has in the most differing ways taken this spiritual

achievement into his heart, where it acts as the indispensable foundation of his spiritual awareness. This is precisely the foundation upon
which all those born afterwards may build, and that enables someone
to present their own independently gained knowledge as the main
content of a lecture. At the same time this reveals the fact that ever
newer insights are indeed arising from the different ways of seeing the
spiritual world, but that these never contradict one another and fit
together like pieces of a puzzle with the statements made by Rudolf
Steiner. This *has* to be so; since only information based on real and
objective insights, and not on the simple repetition of spiritual facts
already condensed into earthly words nor on nice sounding exoteric
theory or deliberation, is always true and to be taken seriously.

Often it even occurs that two spiritual researchers come up with the
same images. How does this happen? Someone who tries to express
something supersensible in language based on the physical senses is
always at the limits of his possibilities. He has to resort quite often to
image-like comparisons to be able to present his ideas. By practising
the exercise in open-mindedness★ the listener can for his or her part
bring an increased receptivity to assist the speaker. Nevertheless much
still remains imperfect. But if we do not bring ourselves to make the
attempt to speak and write imperfectly, if we are afraid of doing so,
then we might as well not say anything to one another. (It goes
without saying that no matter how much tolerance you may show
towards the imperfection of language, a real struggle for the most
fitting description must constantly be taking place). Nevertheless there
is no way of avoiding the fact that in the supersensible world there is
no need for expression in terms of earthly language, which is why
revelations of the supersensible world cannot be translated into earthly
words without some difficulties. The only exception to this are the
mantras, which are a spiritual cosmos of independent and living
spiritual beings compressed into the world of the senses. People from
the most diverse historical periods and the most diverse cultures who
have received esoteric truths from the spiritual world have for this
reason arrived again and again at similar images to express these truths.
This could be symbols like the five or the six-pointed star for repre-

★ Translator's note: One of Rudolf Steiner's basic meditative exercises.

senting the human being on Earth or for the relationship between Heaven and Earth; it could be a real image of spiritual impressions like that of the tree which can be found for example in the ancient Hebrew Menorah, in the Kabbalistic Tree of the Sephiroth, or in Genesis with the Tree of Knowledge and the Tree of Life. There are also quite other possibilities such as numerical series and relationships, or the parables from the Gospels. These examples are intended to clarify how the findings of individual spiritual research can produce similar fruits. In this way some depictions or images may seem peculiarly familiar to the reader although he or she does not know them directly from Rudolf Steiner.

The second reason why this kind of spiritual perception is being spoken about here at all is the circumstance that some people, without being acquainted with the lectures and consequently lacking sufficient basis for making a judgement, have formed for themselves a quite particular opinion of my fate and of my actions. It goes without saying, of course, that they are entitled to their opinion. The opinions being spread which have been formed in this way are however without any serious basis. In this way judgements arise such as: the only use anthroposophical spiritual science has for me is so that I can cope with my fate and the effects of the stigmatization. Or: the fate I am now living through is not the goal of the path of development of Anthroposophy as a science of the spirit. With such kinds of statements my spiritual awareness and my development as a person with the stigmata are to a certain extent placed in opposition to the path of Anthroposophy. Here it is to be stressed once again—and this is repeatedly being said in the lectures—that of course, it is not at all the fate of everyone who is treading the path of Rosicrucian initiation and developing him or herself in the spirit of Anthroposophy to receive the stigmata. It is a completely individual fate; a few things about this are set out in the lectures. Though it must be said that such a fate also does not prevent the person from taking the path of development of spiritual science.

This is why once again specific reference will be made here to the difference between the two kinds of awareness mentioned above. The authentic experience of the events of the life of Christ caused by receiving the stigmata is radically different in its entire nature from the esoteric knowledge *about* the events of Christ's life which is only possible for someone living *after* the development of anthroposophical spiritual science.

It may become clear that the knowledge of spiritual science imparted by Rudolf Steiner has obviously made a fundamental contribution to understanding the phenomena which have occurred; but that which can be called the path of knowledge of spiritual science was central to my life long before receiving the stigmata. I feel in my heart completely immersed in the esoteric truths expressed by Rudolf Steiner, since from an early age I was already aware in a quite natural way of the cosmic home where my being arose. The esoteric truths in the lectures are spoken from the heart. And this heart—irrespective of the stigmata—is my heart.

That is why my efforts are focused only on those esoteric insights which will shed a contemporary light on the descriptions of the historical events of Christ's life. One fact, however, also remains, that the basis for my speaking in public is formed by the merging together in my person of two different ways of spiritual and psychic perception.

Judith von Halle
Berlin, Midsummer 2005

I

CONCERNING THE RELATIONSHIP BETWEEN STIGMATIZATION AND THE RESURRECTION BODY

About the knowledge and reality of the Resurrection of Christ

10 October 2004★

Judith von Halle

Dear Members, dear Friends,

This evening we would like to try and speak about the transformation of the human being—in particular his physical body—through the Christ impulse. In addition we want to examine in a spiritual-scientific way the path of development of the human self†. Rudolf Steiner characterized the Mystery of Golgotha as the birth of the individual human self (see for example the lecture from 7 January 1912, GA 143). Since God's deed on Golgotha, since His sacrifice on the Cross, since He penetrated the depths of matter in order to enable true and clear self-awareness for humans, we are able consciously to understand our individual self, to give it a name and utilize it for our development. Our individual self stands at the beginning of its path of development, it is still quite young. But for the past 125 years it has now been able to awaken, steeled in the light of the spirit, at the side of Michael, who is pointing to us the way back to the highest of all beings. About two thousand years ago this highest of all beings, Christ, gave us a seed of power, which we can stimulate today into growth and into flower by deciding for Him. For Him who first enabled us to choose Him in freedom—as it says in Rudolf Steiner's *Foundation Stone Meditation*:

★ During this lecture reproductions were shown of Giotto's fresco of Francis of Assisi receiving the stigmata (San Francesco, Assisi) and the painting of the Resurrection by Matthias Grünewald (Isenheim Altar, Museum Unterlinden, Colmar).

† Translator's note: The term 'self' or 'individual self' is felt to be a more appropriate translation of the German word *das Ich* than the more literal 'the I'. The German word directly combines the personal, individual sense of the word as well as its universal sense and though this is partly lost, the term 'the self' is nevertheless better for maintaining the flow and sound of the English text.

Where the Gods' eternal goals
Grant the light of cosmic being
To our own self
for willing in freedom

This is the position we are in today. And if we decide for Him in love and humility and have in addition the great karmic 'fortune' of being able to know and study Anthroposophy as a way to understanding His deed, then the result will one day be the transformation of our physical body. A body will be developed that will not just be the bearer of the spirit but spirit itself, or in the words of John, the 'new temple'.

Peter Tradowsky

Dear Members, dear Friends,
In the invitation to this evening's lecture attention was drawn to the fact that particularly this first lecture is based primarily upon Rudolf Steiner's lecture cycle *From Jesus to Christ* (GA 131). So an acquaintance with the lecture cycle, even a study of it, is assumed.

Today we want to report on a specific event that has occurred right in our midst. It is a cosmic event manifesting in Judith von Halle. In Passiontide 2004 the stigmata, the wounds of Jesus Christ, appeared on Judith von Halle.

Before examining this event in the context and with the help of the lecture cycle *From Jesus to Christ*, we shall first describe the phenomena which have occurred.

The stigmata, which appeared in rapid succession, are exactly the way Matthias Grünewald portrayed them in his depiction of the Resurrection from the Isenheim altar in Colmar. The wounds bled especially in the Holy Week and on Good Friday. They bled during Eastertime until the Feast of Whitsun more or less every Friday and since then only sporadically on specific occasions, above all as a result of severe psychological strain. The stigmata, which hurt more or less continuously, have since then remained essentially unaltered. Their peculiarity consists in the fact that they do not become inflamed but neither do they heal.

The stigmatization was accompanied by a radical change in the entire blood system, which, as the physical-spiritual expression of the self, penetrates and connects all the organs and their spheres of activity. In the process, the whole organism is affected by the change, of which two aspects will be mentioned. All sensory perception is intensified and sensory experience expanded. Occasionally something being spoken hundreds of yards away can be heard exactly. The sense of smell can perceive what is happening in another person as he digests his food, it can perceive what had been eaten many hours before, where the food came from, what qualities it had and how it had been prepared.

Quite a drastic change occurred from Maundy Thursday to Good Friday in respect of nutrition. Suddenly without any transition it was completely impossible to eat anything. Every attempt at eating something resulted in symptoms of poisoning. Up to the present the condition of not being able to eat has not changed. It is to be emphasized that the impossibility of eating physical food did not appear as a result of some form of ascetic practices—as the account of what happened shows. The altered body of Judith von Halle, who previously loved cooking and eating, now vehemently refuses any physical food. Only water in limited amounts can be taken. However, despite eating nothing, body weight has not altered in any way.

The reaction to alcohol of her transformed body is remarkable. Even barely measurable quantities, as for example in toothpaste or even the mere smell of alcohol lead to severe symptoms of poisoning.

The stigmatization was accompanied by a certain change in consciousness on the Good Friday and on every following Friday. Judith von Halle will be telling you in the rest of the lecture about her experience arising from the stigmatization, of living through the events of Christ's life retained in the Cosmos.

At this point let it just be said that the whole person is so physically, mentally, emotionally and spiritually present and so completely absorbed while the historical events in Palestine are being lived through, that normal consciousness based on the senses and reason is abandoned.

The dreadful events—lasting many hours—of ill-treatment, torture and finally the Crucifixion and death throes, are in the meantime reflected in the physical body. These drastic and shattering experiences reach their climax in the death of Jesus Christ. But they then continue with the spiritual experience of the so-called Descent into Hell, which Judith von Halle will also be talking about in detail later. But forever counterbalancing the experience of the death on the Cross will be the Resurrection of Christ, shining through and filling the whole soul and strengthening the physical body; will be the meeting with the Saviour of the World 'on the first day of the week ... early, while it was yet dark' (John 20:1).

According to the way of calculating the hours of the day at the time, 'early' means six o'clock in the morning. This refers though to the actual local time in Jerusalem. This time corresponds to four o'clock in the morning Central European time. The Resurrection and all the other similar experiences were in fact experienced here (in Germany) at this time, i.e. roughly two hours earlier.

So much for now about the physical body and the changes brought about by the stigmatization. Now the attempt will be made to approach the phenomena by means of spiritual science. Of course, at first only a few aspects can be considered.

The appropriate mood for a spiritual-scientific approach towards the Mystery of Golgotha can best be created by reading the conclusion to the lecture cycle *From Jesus to Christ*. This is why we have placed at the beginning of our investigation into the Resurrection body these words:

What kind of an act was it?—It was an act of divine love! We must understand that no human feeling is capable of experiencing the intensity of love that was necessary in order for a God to come to a decision for which it had no need, the decision to be active in a human body on the earth. As a result, by an act of love, that event was initiated which is the most important event in human evolu-tion. And when humans will understand God's act of love, when they attempt to experience this act of love as a high ideal compared to which all human acts of love can only appear tiny, then mankind will draw closer to one another through this feeling of inadequacy of human love compared to the divine love which was necessary for the Mystery of Golgotha .... In truth it is indeed possible to visualize the Mount upon which the Cross was raised, that Cross upon which a God hung in a human body, a God who accomplished an act of free will—in other words, an act of love—so that the Earth and humanity can reach their goal. Had not the God who is given the name of the Father God allowed the luciferic influences to be able to approach the human being, he would not have then developed the basis for his freedom of self. This had to be permitted by the Father God. For the sake of freedom the human self had to become entangled in the material world. But now, in order to be freed from this entanglement in matter, the whole love of the Son had to give rise to the act of Golgotha. Only as a result of this has human freedom, full human dignity, first become possible. [...] So we as humans may feel like free beings, but we should not forget that we owe this freedom to an act of God's love. When we think in this way then the following thought shifts into the centre of our feelings: You can achieve human dignity; but the one thing you should not forget is that you owe what you are to Him who restored to you your archetypal human form through the act of salvation on Golgotha. Humanity ought not to be able to embrace the idea of freedom without the idea of salvation through Christ (GA 131, 14 October 1911).

Firstly, we are made aware of God's act of inexhaustible love, which human understanding can and ought to approach without having to unveil the mystery of love or being able to unveil it. Secondly, attention is drawn to the eternal source of human freedom; if the self wishes to take the path of freedom it must relate clearly to this origin. With the help of spiritual science we shall now briefly go into how the phantom body, the Resurrection body, had its first origins on Saturn, how then, after passing through the Sun and Moon phases, this archetypal form was destroyed by the influence of spiritual beings who had remained behind on the Earth (the Fall of Man) and how through Christ and His sacrifice this phantom was renewed. This renewal of the archetypal human physical form is foreshadowed in the trans-formed physical body of Judith von Halle. This transformation, which develops in every spiritually striving person, does not necessarily have to be accompanied by the appearance of the stigmata. The stigmata however, indicate that the transformation corresponds to the renewed phantom.

The Resurrection body, the phantom, is—as explained in the lecture cycle *From Jesus to Christ*—the renewal of the spiritual-physical archetype of the human physical body. This body was a creation of the Spirits of Will, the Thrones, on ancient Saturn as the hierarchy of the Archai were passing through their human stage. They were as a result involved in the creation of human beings in so much as they inserted into the physical basis, for the senses, their potential for being used on the future Earth as instruments of the self. A momentous schism occurred in the hierarchy of the Archai on Saturn, whose effects are of major importance for the present-day development of the human self. For the Archai who remained behind, who we also call 'Asuras', seduce and tempt humans into abject egoism; they are at present the evil spirits of ancient Saturn and are armed with the strongest will to evil. By virtue of this fact, our present-day self development is under constant threat from the effects of this schism.

The physical body, which was created on Saturn, is therefore the oldest and most perfect element of the human being. On the Earth, the Elohim (the Spirits of Form, Spirits of the individual self) in an act of creation, eventually integrated the individual self from out of the substance of their being into the physical body.

The first humans on the Earth, however, had a physical body which was invisible. The true human being is today also invisible and as a result the question arises of how it is that the human has become a visible being. The development to a state of being visible was triggered by the spiritual influence Lucifer exerted upon the human astral body:

> Because the potential control and mastery of mental images by the astral body was aroused in the human astral body, human consciousness was, as a result, stripped of its character as a mere mirror of the cosmos.
>
> The human being became the arbiter of his own knowledge. On the other hand, though, the astral body was the basis for this control (of mental images), and as a result the self, although on a higher level, became constantly dependent on it. As a result the human being was continuously exposed in the future to the influence of a lower element in his nature (GA 13).

Through the desires and passions of his astral body the human being turned more and more away from the influences of the higher spiritual worlds and more and more towards his own being. This disruption of the original harmony, which was however necessary for the development towards the individual self, led consequently to illness and finally to death. On the basis of this inner self-centredness the human being also formed false ideas about the surrounding external world, which is purely spiritual by nature, but which through a fundamental error increasingly appeared to him in a material form. The human being is subject to the illusion of Ahriman in relation to the external world. Initially the human being came under the spiritually seducing influence of Lucifer and as a result finally fell into the clutches of Ahriman. The human being 'now only took in earthly impressions which could be experienced through the inoculated astral element and which had combined with the forces which destroy the physical body. The human being experienced this as a fading away of his physical life. And "Death" appeared as a result, caused by human nature itself' (GA 13). In this way the development of the human being on Earth led to a radical change. The immortal, invisible spiritual archetypal form was destroyed and the human became a mortal, visible and sick being that had become entangled in the darkness and hardness of matter.

This experience in pre-Christian cultures led increasingly to a mood of tragedy. The sublime teachings of the Buddha expressed this resignation towards the Earth: the human being must free himself from earthly suffering in order to be saved. The many different forms of the Mysteries in ancient times were also helpless in face of the physical body's decline. Mankind's awareness of the limits to its own capabilities would have plunged it into despair if the expectation of a future world saviour had not developed. The people of Israel were chosen to create within themselves the bodily and spiritual conditions for receiving the Saviour of the World. The 'I am the I am' was proclaimed in advance by Moses, and his teachings prepared the way for Christ's coming.

Christ's resolve to carry out the deed of love for humanity and the Earth involves the decision to penetrate into the earthly kingdom (*Malchut*), into which no human self could penetrate. This meant on the other hand though that God had to pass through the Crucifixion into death in order to overcome death in death. The renewal of the archetypal form of the physical body, which knows no death, is the goal of the incarnation of God.

By means of the findings of spiritual science imparted by Rudolf Steiner in the lecture cycle *From Jesus to Christ* it has—for the first time in the history of Christianity—become possible to take the first steps towards understanding the Resurrection. Nowadays each individual can feel the compulsion to exert his powers of the spirit in order to come to an initial understanding of the Mystery of Golgotha. Spiritual science can make a significant contribution; but the mystery will never be fully explained, as the way there is as long as the evolution of the Earth, for the mystery of love is inexhaustible.

In order to take the first steps towards understanding the Resurrection, it is first of all necessary to understand correctly the concept of the physical body, which means not remaining at the level of earthly substances and material forces. Rudolf Steiner explains:

The more human clairvoyance develops in our time, however, the more one thing will become clear to humanity: that everything deposited in the physical body as physical substances and forces is not the whole physical body, that this does not even provide the whole form of the physical body. But something else belongs to these substances and forces, which we are obliged, correctly speaking, to call the human 'phantom'. This phantom is the creative form of the human being, a spiritual web which shapes the physical substances and forces so that they come into the form which confronts us on the physical plane as the human being. A sculptor cannot create a statue if he takes some marble or some other material and begins wildly hammering away, pieces breaking off in a manner befitting the nature of the material. But the sculptor has to have thoughts which he impresses into the material. For the human body the thought is also present, but as the material of the human body is not marble or plaster, it is not present in the same way as the artist's thoughts are present, but as a real thought in the outer world: as the phantom. What the sculptor impresses into his material is impressed as the phantom of the physical body into the substances of the Earth, which we see after death being laid in the grave or being cremated. The phantom belongs to the physical body, it is the remaining part of the physical body and is more important than the outer substances; for the outer substances are basically nothing more than something which is loaded into the net-like structure of the human form, like apples loaded onto a cart. The phantom is something important! The substances which decompose after death are essentially those we also encounter outside in nature, only they have been caught up by the human form (GA 131, 10 October 1911).

The Resurrection becomes understandable on the basis of this comprehensive concept of the physical body:

The death that this one human being—who was the bearer of the Christ—experienced, was such a death that after three days, that part of the physical body which in human beings is mortal, had to disappear and out of the grave arose that body which is the bearer of the forces of the physical-material elements. [...] It is possible for the human constitution to retain these forces which were resurrected at that time, in the same way as his physical organization, as a result of the luciferic forces at the beginning of the Earth, retained the Adam nature (GA 131, 10 October 1911).

Paul saw quite clearly in the Resurrection the distinctive core of Christianity. The encounter with Christ, which he had on the way to Damascus, the concrete experience of the Resurrection, formed the foundation of his entire teachings:

What he experienced was what he knew can only be experienced when the Scriptures had first been fulfilled: a complete human phantom, the supersensory form of a human body risen from the grave existing for the first time in the spiritual atmosphere of the Earth. He had seen it! This is what had appeared to him on the way to Damascus and convinced him: He is here! He is risen! The phantom is there! The phantom which can only come from Him, and which can be seen by every human individual who seeks a relationship with Christ, is there! (GA 131, 12 October 1911).

Christianity stands and falls with the Resurrection and the crisis of Christianity is that there is little understanding or none at all of the Resurrection.

The teachings of Paul are the consequence of his knowledge of the Resurrection. We can trace the natural line of descent back to the first human being, Adam:

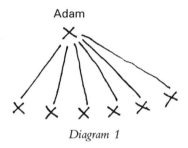

Diagram 1

The new unity of mankind, which can be created by Christians, proceeds from the Resurrected Christ, from the second, the new Adam:

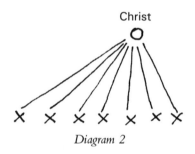

Diagram 2

If you want to become a Christian in the true sense, you have to imagine that something can arise in you which is able to live within you and about which you are obliged to say that just as all humans can trace connecting lines to the physical body of the first Adam, so you as well can draw spiritual lines from this something living within you to a second Adam, to Christ, and in fact to the Christ who rose from the grave on the third day. So Paul demanded from all who call themselves Christians that they inwardly develop something which is truly within them and which leads, in the same way the corruptible body leads back to Adam, to that which arose from the grave on the third day (GA 131, 10 October 1911).

It is essential to understand this diagram and these words of Rudolf Steiner correctly. On the first Easter Sunday morning the *one*

Resurrection body had actually been created by Christ and He appeared to Mary Magdalene and the disciples in this Resurrection body. In the further progress of humanity this one original Resurrection body was replicated according to the principle of spiritual economy; in other words, the individual human self which begins to receive Christ into itself, puts on the phantom and in this process the phantom is replicated and individualized. As the renewed archetypal form of the physical body the phantom will be the 'garment' of the self in a more perfect and ideal way than any material-physical body stemming from the line of heredity can be. The Christ Being provides humans with the power to develop their individual self, but also at the same time the possibility to transform, to spiritualize and individualize the sheaths of their being. To this extent it is not just a 'renewal of the phantom', as the individual form of the Resurrection body newly created by Christ surpasses the old Adam. It goes without saying that the process of individualization and of putting on the phantom can only be conceived as one which continues over many incarnations until the end of the evolution of the Earth. This law was clearly expressed by Rudolf Steiner in his *Occult Science: An Outline*:

> Since the Christ event humans who raise themselves to the Mystery of Christ can carry over into the spiritual world what they have gained from the world of the senses. And this flows back again from the spiritual world into the material sensory world by humans bringing with them when they reincarnate what they have developed of the Christ impulse in the spiritual world between death and a new birth (GA 13).

The transformation caused by putting on the phantom applies at first to the physical body, but extends to all the sheaths. At the Last Supper on Maundy Thursday Christ performed with the disciples an initial stage in the transformation of the normal process of nutrition. Humans will be reconnected by means of the Resurrection body with the karmic stream of nutrition which builds the substances in the human being. As the original phantom increasingly lost its strength, the necessity arose of physically and materially nourishing a body which had become material, in other words, normal physical nutrition can be traced back to a weakening of the phantom. Rudolf Steiner expressed the facts as follows: 'One way of comprehending to some extent this degeneration is that from the beginning of human development this phantom was actually meant to remain untouched by the material elements absorbed as food by the human being from the mineral, plant and animal kingdoms. But it did not remain untouched' (GA 131, 14 October 1911).

In this way, the astonishing fact of someone living without eating or drinking, which for many is extremely difficult to understand and indeed often not even acknowledged, is shown not to be an illness but instead an expression of a new form of health. Such statements, however, should not lead to a fanatical asceticism which can never reach its goal. Attaining the goal, the constant transformation of the human body and its physical organization, requires, as has been pointed out, patience, and ultimately it takes an act of grace as well. The spiritual-scientific understanding of nutrition requires a certain generosity of soul, even a certain portion of humour, but no one ought to allow it to spoil their appetite.

The question is constantly being asked whether stigmatization must follow when we put on the phantom in the sense of the teachings of Paul. Once again this is to be unequivocally and emphatically denied. Stigmatization is an individual life situation determined by karma, which presents a challenge to humans but does not mean that in the future every person will bear the stigmata.

The development of the individual self through the integration of the Christ impulse is a gradual, stage-by-stage process of fusion with the Resurrection body as the renewed phantom. This happens in an absolutely individual way and can remain outwardly hidden. In this context Rudolf Steiner explicitly mentions on the one hand that 'even today for many things the full truth cannot be presented'. On the other hand it is emphatically stressed that the truth of modern initiation lies precisely in the putting on of the phantom: 'To a certain extent the same thing is now attained only by somewhat different means. Through initiation an individual is nowadays able to experience that a bond of attraction is created between the human being, to the extent he is incarnated in a physical body, and that which arose as the actual archetype of the physical body out of the grave from Golgotha' (GA 131, 14 October 1911).

The teachings of Paul about the first and the second Adam are expanded and deepened fundamentally in the knowledge of spiritual science. They are valid on a general level. Stigmatization, for the person affected as well as for his surroundings, is in comparison something extremely personal. For whatever these surroundings— that means the people who are aware of what has happened—may think of this phenomenon, they are karmically connected with it.

Judith von Halle

We have now heard some details about the phantom. This so-called phantom body is a changed, a transformed physical body. And this transformed physical body is also capable of having sensory perceptions. These sensory perceptions are in no way inferior to the sensory perceptions of a non-transformed physical body. These perceptions are of persons, places and events which lie thousands of miles away or in far distant times. For me my new bodily organization is connected with the historical events in Palestine two thousand years ago.

As you know, no historical evidence exists for the life, the acts, the death and the Resurrection of Christ. It seems to be the case, however, that time and again throughout the course of world history there have been individuals who by witnessing these events with their senses are able themselves to be also living witnesses to this act of the Son of God. Their witness is more convincing than for example a death sentence written on papyrus, as these individuals can relay to the people of their time an account of these events absolutely accurate in every detail. Their perceptions are more comprehensive than any document which has come down to us can ever be, in fact even richer in details than the Gospels, because, as already said, these are actual sensory perceptions. We know of accounts of these events from other stigmatics. We, however, have come to the conclusion that it would make more sense to collect my own experiences together and bring them first to paper before comparing them with statements from other stigmatics.

When I speak therefore of sensory perception this is exactly what is meant. I will now speak to you from my own experience. Please imagine undertaking a journey in time which results in you being transferred to another age with all the everyday capabilities of awareness and perception you possess at this moment sitting in the hall and hearing my voice, seeing the curtain behind me, perhaps smelling the floor cleaner, feeling the arm of your neighbour. My perception of the events in Palestine two thousand years ago also includes the languages spoken there at the time—mostly Aramaic, alongside Greek, Roman Latin and Hebrew—and includes, as well, the religious ceremonies of the time, the social structures and the way of thinking, which was totally different to the way of thinking we are familiar with today. At this point the personality of Pilate can be mentioned, whose way of acting was completely characteristic for his time. I also perceive other details of everyday life—such as customs of dress, food and drink, architecture, landscape, weather, even the constellations of the stars or the celebration of the festivals of the year which the people of the time experienced quite intensively, as is shown in the preparations for the Passover (*Pesach, Passah*) in the course of which the Last Supper took place.

The perception of these events began for me in the Holy Week and the Easter Week of this year (2004) and concentrated on the experience of the Crucifixion, the Death, the Descent into Hell and the Resurrection of Christ. Since this time the perceptions have been continuously expanding, you could say, in a radial manner. In other words the fullness of details has increased and my ability to witness events now stretches to those events occurring before the Crucifixion and after the Resurrection. Up until now I have also been able to witness events like the Last Supper, the night in the Garden of Gethsemane, Jesus being taken prisoner, His scourging and the bartering over His death, the judgement, the arduous road to Golgotha, the putting together of the Cross, the nailing to the Cross, the erection of the Cross, the endless agony of Jesus on the Cross and—in spite of all this agony—the loving words of forgiveness for those who abused and tortured Him. I would like to add at this point that the agonies which preceded the Crucifixion were already so enormous that it is a real miracle to me that Christ survived through to the Crucifixion. Please also take into account that we are dealing here with a capacity for suffering increased to the highest degree, as the Sun Logos, the Son of God, had only been living for three years in a human body and did not know physical pain the way a normal human being does. The closer He came to death, the deeper He penetrated matter, the more unbearable His agony became, the more He became completely human. But even in these moments it was possible for Him in His divine capacity to feel and express compassion for His taunters and tormentors.

The perceptions then expanded as well to the moment of death and to the time afterwards, as well as to the penetration into the abyss of the Earth—'descended into the Kingdom of Death'. During this time everything of an ahrimanic nature was laid in chains by Christ descending into the depths. This experience is different to sensory perception. It is a form of perception in the spiritual-pyschic realm free of the body. The difference between these two ways of experiencing was gone into in detail in the Introduction. Afterwards followed the perception of the Resurrection which I was permitted to witness with the two kinds of perception just mentioned. The Resurrection begins with the experience of the transformation of the body of the Earth: a light that penetrated as drops of blood into the Earth and now spreads out, rises up and in the morning darkness breaks out of the transformed body of the Earth. It is the one true ray of divine light and power, which earthly words cannot describe. The life-force emanating from the Resurrection strengthens me inwardly so much that I can be outwardly nourished by it.

If you imagine a set of scales and in the one weighing pan are the agonies and the death of Christ and in the other the Resurrection, you should not think that the weighing pans would be balanced. The event of the Resurrection carries so much more weight and significance than death. Everything alive within us springs from it. It is the life-sustaining power, not just for me but also for each one of you, and it occurs anew in us everyday. This is the gift of the Resurrection for each one of us.

I would like to say a few more words concerning the decision to present these events. It was not easy for me to address myself to an audience, as such a presentation involves making public intimate facts of a spiritual and psychological as well as a bodily nature, and laying these facts before people I do not know personally at all. And yet there are two reasons on which I based my decision to override my personal concerns. Seven months have now gone by since the stigmata first appeared. This period of time may seem short to one or the other of you. For me these months, during which I was confronted daily with the effects of this phenomenon, seemed like several years. The reason for this may lie in the sensitization of my body already mentioned, by means of which—also through the pain from the stigmata—the rudiments of the immense suffering of the Christ Being for the sake of humanity and its fate passed daily before my eyes. One could also say that with each passing day life has an even greater impact on the soul.

Despite my efforts, in these months it soon became apparent to me that it was impossible to hide completely the appearance of the stigmata and the phenomena connected with them. The alternative would have been complete isolation, which as a consequence would have meant giving up my job, abandoning my work within the anthroposophical community as well as fleeing from friends and family. This however seemed to me like fleeing from my own life. Furthermore, I soon had to recognize that the meaning of the phantom body becoming visible in the stigmata was obvious, namely, to be visible. It became evident that the attempt to hide completely and for as long a time as possible those stigmata appearing on exposed parts of the body, and the fact of not eating or drinking anything, would be a denial of precisely this wish of the phantom to be revealed by becoming visible. I clearly felt my inner yearning over and again for anonymity and inconspicuousness but I had to admit to myself that the inner calling I had heard from early on, to do something for the being coming to expression in these stigmata, had to be obeyed.

One reason why I have decided on this internal presentation of the events is to prevent speculative, unobjective and sensational accounts from third persons reaching you—in other words this is my attempt to provide a worthy explanation of the events. The second reason though is that I am now ready to bear witness with all my strength for this gift which has been given us through Christ's act of love.

What concerns me the most though with regard to all the details presented in the lectures is that the Being who reveals Himself through the stigmata, through the bodily transformation, will be seen in the forefront and not my person. This will not always be easy as the wounds are indeed appearing on my person. But I beg you to distinguish between pure self-promotion and the attempt to describe spiritual facts. This concern goes along with the request not to consider me an individual who has been struck by a sheer miracle, for, as has already been pointed out today, all these phenomena are perfectly explainable with the help of anthroposophical knowledge, and do not represent a pathological condition but point to the future bodily organization of the human being. This transformed bodily organiza-tion involves the body, soul and spirit and is caused by the Christian trait of *compassion*, of experiencing another's suffering. Any changes of a physical nature proceed from an impulse of the spirit and the soul. And the catalyst for this transformation is to a large extent compassion, which nowadays counts for little. In fact you have to justify feeling compassion, as it is often negatively classified as a psycho-pathological condition. In connection with this I would like to remind you of the words of Rudolf Steiner from his lecture cycle on the Apocalypse (GA 104a). There he states that the soul of future humans can only be in a state of fulfilment when the last fellow human on Earth no longer has to feel any pain. This basic fact of human development Rudolf Steiner brings to expression in his saying of the Good Samaritan from 1 December 1914 (GA 157), which I would like to quote to you:

> As long as *you* feel the pain
> Which avoids me,
> Christ acting in the Being of the Cosmos
> Is unrecognized;
> For the spirit stays weak
> If it is only able to feel the pain
> In its own body.

Nothing could be further from my mind than to evangelize to people. No one should ever feel compelled to anything in any way whatso-ever. Something is indeed coming towards you—and I take the liberty of saying that the spiritual world certainly does not arrange such a visible demonstration of itself for the single individual affected, but for those around this person—but you are not compelled to anything. I already referred at the beginning of the evening to freedom, that archetypal Christian element of conscious, free choice. This also implies, of course, the possibility of not wanting to address the topic or to associate oneself any further with it, with the drawing near of the spirit. This also is then right for the person concerned, as he has made a conscious and free decision which will be accepted by the spiritual world.

I am not talking to you about this, therefore, in order to achieve a particular effect and certainly not to be sensational, as this only distracts from the silent, intimate encounter with the Christ Being. Rather it has become a responsibility of mine not to withhold the revelation of this visible spirit at least from those people who are struggling together with me for knowledge, namely you, my dear anthroposophical friends.

And please believe me when I say, the Christ Being is speaking quite personally to you. The warmth of this light glowing deep down in us can be felt from time to time. Through our striving for knowledge and through the sympathy of our hearts we can let this light, the Sun of Christ, rise up in us to become a blazing flame. This is Christ's gift of love.

I will be constantly striving to bring home to you that the workings of Christ on me are part of His love for *all* mankind

Finally we would kindly ask you to use the information presented in a responsible and careful manner.

The significance of the phantom, the Resurrection body, for an understanding of the human being

7 November 2004

Peter Tradowsky

Dear Members, dear Friends,

We are not of the opinion that putting on the Resurrection body in the sense of Paul must lead to receiving the stigmata. But because this point of view keeps on coming up again and again in conversations, it is to be expressly and emphatically stressed once again that there is no basis for this way of thinking. Stigmatization is an individual karmic event only to be understood in terms of individual karma and is therefore not to be generalized. It has already been mentioned that the preparation for receiving the phantom (as Rudolf Steiner expresses it) is a highly individual process stretching over many incarnations and leads by means of the replication of the one original Resurrection body to each individual self receiving its ideal body as the bearer of the self.

Stigmatization, however, can be understood as a particular expression of the revelation of the Resurrection body, above all because of the radical transformation of the physical body occurring in the process. This transformation is especially seen in the body no longer needing physically to eat or drink anything.

For the moment the spiritual-scientific concept of the Resurrection—as Rudolf Steiner observed—can only be half the truth. The spiritual-scientific concept of the Resurrection is an infinite, inexhaustible concept. It paves the way for our understanding for it connects the beginning and the end of the Earth, the Alpha and Omega, through the deed of Christ on Golgotha. The physical body was originally an energy form, a 'real thought in the outside world' (GA 131, 10 October 1911), that means a reality-creating thought. Through the influence of Lucifer and Ahriman this has degenerated, has been destroyed. Only through the Resurrection restoring the

original principle of human evolution can the development of the
individual self continue. Through the Resurrection of Christ a new
element has been added to humanity, an imperishable body, to which
every individual self can relate.

May I stress again in relation to the stigmata that those stigmata
temporarily appearing at the fourth stage of the Christian path of
initiation, the Crucifixion, have to be distinguished absolutely from
the permanent, karmically determined stigmata. They have, of
course, the same origin, but are obviously related to it in different
ways. If one takes Giotto's depiction of the stigmatization of Francis
of Asissi seriously, it can be said that Christ gives and takes away the
stigmata for reasons of His own. Basically all stigmatics have felt this
way, which has led to both sympathy as well as rejection from their
surroundings.

The phenomenon of stigmatization is inexplicable for present-day
materialistic science and medicine and has to be denied as its presence
does not just shake the foundations of their world-view, but destroys
them. This denial is the logical consequence of the complete separation of nature and spirit, or rather the postulated non-existence of
spirit. In contrast, spiritual science shows how the human being and
the Earth have evolved together from the spiritual world. The words
given by Goethe to the Chancellor and Archbishop (*Faust* II, Act I,
The Hall of Thrones, trans. George Madison Priest), the representative
of the Church view, are the paradigmatic expression of this:

Nature and mind—don't talk to Christians thus!
Men burn up atheists, fittingly,
Because such speeches are most dangerous.
Nature is sin, and mind is devil,
They nurture doubt in doubt they revel,
Their hybrid, monstrous progeny.

For this reason spiritual science, as a science of the comprehensive
reality of spirit and nature, is also called upon to make a contribution
to an understanding of stigmatization. A broad outline shall here be
provided in relation to the transformation of sensory perception and
the state of non-eating of any physical food. A fundamental require-
ment for this is the knowledge that Ahriman's power has been con-

strained by the Mystery of Golgotha. Rudolf Steiner writes in *Occult Science: An Outline* concerning this:

> At the moment the Golgotha event occurred, the other capacity was introduced into humanity by which the influence of Ahriman can be turned to good. The human being can now take with him through the gate of death that from life which will free him from isolation in the spiritual world. The event from Palestine is central not only for the physical development of mankind but also for the remaining worlds to which the human being belongs. And with the fulfilment of the 'Mystery of Golgotha', with the suffering of the 'Death on the Cross', Christ appeared in that world in which human souls were to be found after death and put the power of Ahriman in its place (GA 13).

For the moment we will focus on showing how a change in the material physical body is initiated.

Normally the senses are looked upon as substantiating the material aspect of the world. Yet this is nothing other than an ahrimanic illusion arising from the fact that it is hidden from the human being how, with the element of will active in his senses, he is rooted in reality, which is spiritual-physical. The modern, conscious and rational human lives completely in the element of awareness in the senses, which he falsely believes only convey abstract information. Even though the most recent research into the senses increasingly shows this to be an error, up until now a totally different way of understanding the activity of the senses has primarily only been possible through the spiritual science of Rudolf Steiner. In short this can all be found summed up in the following sentence in Schiller's *Aesthetic Letters*: 'The way to the spirit for man is found in the senses'. By means of normal, conscious sensory perception, where the senses are directed outwards, something like the outer side of the spiritual world is perceived, which Ahriman leads humans to believe is the only thing that exists. In present-day civilization this illusion is strengthened by the technical media in so far as they are only capable of reproducing this outer side. When, however, the human being stands facing reality *in nature and mankind*, then the processes of will in the senses unite him with the perceived qualities of the world. This activity of the will has been cloaked in the deepest darkness of the subconscious by the ahrimanic influence, it is forgotten, it can be denied precisely because it is not consciously experienced. Through spiritual knowledge, through spiritual exercises, an awakening begins, a becoming aware of these roots of the activity of the senses in the reality of spirit and nature, in other words, the human being becomes aware that he is living with his will in the spiritual world—something of which he is otherwise unconscious. In his lecture: 'Man's Twelve Senses in Relation to Imagination, Inspiration and Intuition' (GA 199, 8 August 1920) Rudolf Steiner emphasized particularly this aspect. The deepening of the sense of sight, for instance, leads to imagination, a process which played a decisive role in Goethe's discovery of the archetypal plant—which is an imagination. Sensory appearance becomes transparent for spiritual reality. When the doorway of the sense of hearing opens we arrive at inspiration. By means of the sense of self we are able to reach the sphere of intuition tinged with the being of the spiritual outer world. This is in no way a matter of clairvoyance in the normal sense but of a deepened experience of becoming aware of the spiritual reality living in the world experienced by the senses.

The changes in the activities of the senses through stigmatization proceed in the direction here mentioned. The outer side of the spiritual world becomes more or less transparent. The underlying qualities are expressed more strongly and clearly, because the awareness has increased of the reality in which all humans live. So a part—not all—of the astonishing phenomena becomes understandable. These changes in the activities of the senses are to be seen in connection with the radical transformation of the blood system, for as the physical expression of the individual self the blood is the will working unconsciously in all the senses. Stigmatization in this respect also leads to a more conscious experience of the qualities of the senses.

Again and again one can experience the bewilderment, shock and disbelief of people when faced with the situation of someone living without eating anything, arising from the stigmatization. It appears incomprehensible that the transformed body vehemently refuses every outer form of nutrition. This is an attitude that is easy to understand on the one hand but on the other hand is nothing other than the result of real materialism. Again the findings of spiritual science can lead to an initial understanding of the phenomenon. In the third lecture of the lecture cycle *Study of Man* Rudolf Steiner details, for instance, how 'psychological knowledge' suffers 'from the after-effects of the Church dogma, established in 869 AD, which obscured an older view based on instinctive knowledge of the human as a being composed of body, soul and spirit'. A threefold being was replaced by a twofold being. But dualism cannot lead to a comprehensive understanding embracing the whole human being: 'You cannot come to a real understanding of the being of man at all if dualism is the only valid and comprehensive approach' (GA 293, 23 August 1919).

Secondly Rudolf Steiner refers in this lecture to the 'major error' to be found in the law of the conservation of energy or force, a law which has been raised to universal validity:

> What is this law of the conservation of energy or force seen in the larger context of a cultural and historical point of view? It is in general the greatest obstacle to understanding the human being. Since as soon as you are of the opinion that forces are never being newly created, you can never gain any knowledge of the true being of man. This true being of man is based precisely on the fact that new forces are constantly being created by it. Indeed, under the circumstances in the world in which we are living, man is the only being in which new forces and—as we will be hearing later—even new substances are being created (GA 293, 23 August 1919). Rudolf Steiner adds as emphasis that this law 'immediately extinguishes all true understanding if you are wishing to approach the human being'.

The path leading to the place in the human being where forces and substances are created anew, will be described here briefly. The human being comprehends the elements of death and dying in the processes of Nature with his ideas conveyed to him by the dead intellect, bound up to the brain. The living will comprehends through the senses, which, as explained above, live with their active will element in the surroundings, active forces and beings, which in truth are the spiritual world. The spiritual-physical nutrition of the human being is caused as well by this will-process of the senses, as will be gone into in more detail later. With these two polar processes, however, the being of

Man is not fully comprehended. Which is why Rudolf Steiner goes on
to say:

> Above these two elements—the comprehension of that which is
> dead by the intellect and comprehension of that which is living, is in
> a state of becoming by the will—there exists in the human some-
> thing which only he and no other earthly being carries within itself
> from birth until death. This is pure thinking, that thinking which is
> not based on external nature but based only on that supersensible
> element which exists in the human being himself, which makes him
> into an autonomous being, into something beyond the worlds
> existing below death and above life. Accordingly, if one wishes to
> talk about human freedom, one has to keep in mind this autono-
> mous element in man, this pure thinking, free of the senses, in
> which the will also lives (GA 293, 23 August 1919).

As will be shown later, this autonomous element in man can be related
to the Resurrection and the Resurrection body. What the human
being during his life integrates into his body from out of this autonomous element, will keep the Earth alive as a being when the human
gives his body to the Earth at death. The human being carries within
himself, through this autonomous element, a cosmic spiritual process
for the Earth and as a citizen of the Earth he hands over with his body
the fruits of this labour to the Earth: 'Without human corpses the
Earth as a result would have been dead long ago'.

The polar forces of the nerves and the blood are active in the human
being between birth and death. The tension formed between these
two poles produces, in connection with the autonomous element in
man, new forces and substances: 'What then actually takes place in the
being of man? There exists on the one hand the bone-nerve system,
and on the other hand the blood-muscle system. Their working
together is constantly creating new substances and forces. The Earth is
saved from death as a result of new substances and forces being created
in the human being himself'. The blood induces 'through contact
with the nerves the creation of new substances and forces' (GA 293, 23
August 1919).

If we take this path towards a spiritually extended knowledge of the
human being, the non-eating state accompanying stigmatization

becomes understandable. Indeed one can say that the findings of Rudolf Steiner, which are often received with obvious scepticism, even a total lack of understanding, are confirmed by the physical reality of stigmatization, visible to the eyes. For how else can one explain the preservation of a body whose substances and forces, which should have wasted away months ago, actually continue physically and materially to exist, for neither the form nor the weight or the organs are outwardly changed. To this extent the state of non-eating represents a phenomenon which to a significant degree can be understood by spiritual science and is, precisely for this reason, a witness to the fact that it truly comprehends the reality of the human being.

The non-eating state from stigmatization has nothing to do with fasting or any other exercises for transforming human nutrition, such as the so-called 'Living on Light'. Stigmatization is not caused by a human intellectual decision within one single incarnation. One essential difference characterizing stigmatization is the fact that the stigmatized body cannot ingest any physical food. This food acts like a poison in the body, and the body of a stigmatic who has been force-fed would be destroyed by the food. All four constituent elements of the being of Man (physical body, etheric body, astral body and the self) are completely transformed by stigmatization and the source for this transformation lies in the events of the Passion and the Resurrection.

Because it appears in connection with stigmatization the spiritual-physical process of nutrition mentioned here, based on the ingestion of spiritual food, should not be misunderstood as something belonging exclusively to the phenomenon of stigmatization. It lies at the foundation—even if buried deeply—of every existing human being and will play an ever larger role in the future development of the human being. This will be made clearer by means of some references to the story of the Grail. Spiritual science refers to itself as a 'science of the Grail' and has as a result a special relationship to everything connected with the Grail (cf. 'The Present and the Future Evolution of the World and of Mankind', Chapter VI in *Occult Science*, GA 13). The Grail story can be traced back to Joseph of Arimathea and Nicodemus, who asked Pilate for permission to take the body of Christ down from the Cross and to lay it in the grave, which was granted them. In the French Grail tradition, the Grail is the chalice used at the Last Supper and at the same time the vessel in which the blood from the Saviour's wounds was collected. It is sufficient here to draw attention to the fact that this blood which was collected did not flow into the Earth, but was received and looked after by humans. In this Grail tradition, a direct relationship to the events on Golgotha is established through the blood in the chalice. For Wolfram von Eschenbach, the Grail is a stone whose power is renewed each Good Friday by a small white host brought to it by a dove. Both Grail traditions therefore are clearly connected with the Mystery of Golgotha, and—without going into more detail here into the relationship and its secrets—it is understandable that the Grail would be unthinkable without the Resurrection of Christ, without the Easter event. This can be especially seen in the properties which the Grail possesses. The Phoenix burns to ashes on the Grail stone, but the ashes rapidly restore him to life as though he were born again, and he shines radiant and beautiful. Wolfram von Eschenbach then emphasizes that the Grail has the same effect on humans: 'The stone confers such power to men, that flesh and bones are soon made young again'. Also its miraculous food-giving properties are brought about through the power the Grail receives from the dove on Good Friday. The stone receives 'a special power to bestow every form of good-smelling food and drink on Earth, like the perfection of Paradise, I mean: everything *the Earth* may produce'. Here the Easter event is understood in a subtle way as the creation of a new Paradise from which the Earth and mankind will live. This can be seen in the account of the Grail feast when one realizes that the Grail feast is a description of a hidden, unconscious process occurring in a mysterious nocturnal sphere. In the Grail feast we are able to understand the spiritual-physical process of nutrition which enables on a daily basis the physical-material existence of mankind. By means of this spiritual process of nutrition occurring in the subconscious depths of the will, with which every human is living in the substance of the spiritual world, the human being shares in the Grail process, which is an expression of the truth of the Resurrection.

Wolfram von Eschenbach relates the Grail feast in a unique manner to the individual human self. The Grail does not provide one and the same meal for everyone, but instead each one receives individually what he needs: '. . . for whatever each one stretched out his hand, and that he found placed in front of him warm fare, cold fare, new fare, old fare, from tame animals and from wild animals. There has never been such a thing, many would certainly like to object. But whoever speaks so errs in his disapproval. For the Grail was the ripe fruit of blessedness, such an *abundance of Earthly sweetness*, almost equalling to what is said of the Kingdom of Heaven'. The translation cannot convey the profound wisdom and the exquisite humour of this passage. But anyone who is willing can feel the mystery of the feeding of the individual self and the individual form it takes. Emanating from the Grail is the love which keeps, strengthens and bears the individual self as an individual self.

Through contemplating the Grail feast a feeling can be developed for the spiritual force which makes the incarnation of the individual self possible. Something appears through stigmatization which is active in all humans. It certainly does not have to appear always in this form, but it is connected with the future nutrition and health of all mankind.

Judith von Halle

Dear Members, dear Friends,
We have heard something about the appearance of the stigmata and about their connection with the Resurrection body, which Rudolf Steiner calls the phantom body. In December we want to turn our attention to the transformation or the expansion of consciousness that occurred with the appearance of the stigmata. In today's lecture we want to devote some time to the phenomena from the point of view of a general understanding of the human being. The fact that a transformation of the bodily organization has also occurred with the appearance of the stigmata and with the expansion of spiritual experience is almost a scientific and medical indication of the initial stage of development of the phantom.

Unfortunately today we can again only cover a few aspects. Knowledge of the human being has many aspects which interconnect with one another so extensively because they are related to the whole organism and not just to one part. However, in order to give at least an indication of their complexity I will single out and briefly describe a few main areas.

I ought to add that my descriptions are based on my own very personal experiences which I will be trying to treat in the light of spiritual science as objectively as possible. This should be possible as most of the changes bring a certain spiritual objectivity with them by reason of their origin.

I would like to cover the changes occurring in three main areas of the bodily organization this evening: the area of the senses, of the blood and of the metabolism (nutrition).

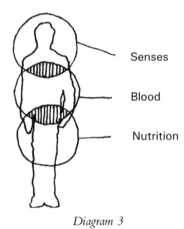

Diagram 3

Among the most difficult topics in Rudolf Steiner's works belongs without a doubt his theory of perception. As all the senses are affected by the changes arising from the development of the phantom body, I can only make a few short comments today on the subject, which I do not claim to be exhaustive. I would like to provide a few examples in relation to the sense of sight, the sense of hearing and the sense of smell.

First of all it is the case that all the senses have become highly refined. As soon as the functions of the old physical body recede and the new body begins to replace them, the senses are refined so intensely in a smooth transition that they no longer belong to the Earth. The activities of the senses expand—precisely as a consequence of this refinement—to the utmost extent, and then switch over into the super-physical. This results in the temporary loss of sensory perception in favour of supersensible perception.

This can be illustrated more concretely using the sense of sight as an example. Instead of the external bodily appearance of a human being, with clothes, hair, eye-colour etc., now his inner formative being, his formative life forces are perceivable. Rudolf Steiner calls this the life body or etheric body. This life body then is not just perceivable in humans, but also in everything that grows, everything that is alive, and everything that is decaying. A quotation from Friedrich Schiller (from: *The Ideal and Life*) proves that he too perceived these formative spiritual forces:

> Only the body is proper for those powers
> who weave the dark fate.
> But free from every sway of time,
> the playmate of blessed natures
> transforms in the meadows of light above,
> Like a God among the Gods, the Form.

A fact is also now perceived that seems quite peculiar to normal perception, that a woman, for example, possesses a masculine life body. If this were not the case then you would have no human being standing before you. The astral form of the human being is brought back into balance by developing a masculine life body in a feminine physical body. The spiritual being of man—irrespective of which sex he outwardly belongs to—is always neutral or unaffected by this.

It is also possible in such a state of perception to observe a person's pulsing, flowing soul forces which, alongside expressing his present emotional state, identify him as a distinctive personality. It is perfectly possible in the normal condition of sensory perception to mistake the identity of someone known to us when seen for example from a distance or from behind. This can never be the case in the condition of transformed perception. This form of perception is not impaired when one closes one's eyes—on the contrary. That which is visible to supersensible eyes always emanates its own light. No outer sun has to shine on it for it to be visible. It shows itself just as it is.

It goes without saying that integrity and an absolutely robust psychological constitution without any egoistic tendencies have to underlie such a form of perception. Although I must add that in my case this kind of imaginative perception did not first arise with the occurrence of the stigmata. At the most I was more able to control the perceptions.

Now what is therefore special about the phantom in relation to the senses? You can approach this phenomenon by focusing on the above mentioned 'expansion' of the senses. The sense of smell is refined, is expanded to such an extent that it is possible, for example, to identify the ingredients of creams, as well as food that someone ate the previous day, or the increased level of iron in the blood of another person, the altered smell of his blood being perspired through the skin. The transformation of the sense of hearing is expressed not just in the switching over to supersensible perception at the inspirational level of 'tones' and spiritual-psychic 'sounds', but also once again in its extreme state of expansion. It can happen that conversations are heard through doors, walls, indeed even in other houses.

The actual characteristic of the phantom body in relation to the senses lies in this extreme state of 'expansion'. This manifests itself in the fact that the activity of the senses is not limited by the bodily organization nor by the etheric body, but occurs directly in the phantom body. This can, in contrast to the etheric body, separate itself from the physical body without destroying in the process the physical existence of the human being. This phantom body, which is a spiritual body—Rudolf Steiner also describes it as a 'real thought in the outside world' (GA 131, 10 October 1911)—is not subject to the laws of either space or time. Now in this spacelessness and time-lessness of the spiritual world it can use the essence of sensory perception; it becomes the creator, the giver-of-life to this essence of the senses. This archetype of the senses, existing as a real idea in the outer world, the actual 'essence' of the senses, is at least as exact as sensory perception in the physical body. This means, when applied to the sense of sight, that the visual sensory experience can happen without the optical instruments of the normal physical body. The sensory optical impressions arise then solely through the physical formative forces of the phantom body. As a result, each single sensory perception can occur over distances of thousands of miles or even in another time.

In order to approach doing justice to this subject one further lecture alone would be necessary at least. Not even all the phenomena which have appeared up until now have been by any means adequately identified.

I would therefore like to move on to the second main area, to the blood. As blood is 'a very special fluid' (J.W.Goethe, *Faust*, V), pervading all areas of the body, it is obviously also connected to the sphere of the senses. (This can be indicated by the overlapping of both circles in diagram 3 and by an example.) Nerve and sensory activity is in the case of normal sensory perception in a normal state of consciousness interwoven with the blood. Sense perceptions extend through the nerves into the blood. That which the human experiences through this relationship can be characterized as an indirectly perceived connection with his assumed external world. The senses create a kind of smoke-screen in the face of the spiritual world. In this way it has become possible for man to distance himself from other physical objects and living beings. He is able to say to himself: there stands a tree and I stand here. The tree is outside of me.

This penetration of the activity of the nerves and the senses into the blood was absolutely essential for the attainment of human self-awareness. But we are now living at a time when we have all developed this self-awareness to perfection and are now able to carry it back up into the higher spiritual worlds. By freeing himself through meditation (or, as in this case, through the permanent reshaping of his sensory and blood systems) from this penetration, by drawing therefore the activity of his nerves out of the blood, the human being annuls the distancing of himself from his outer world just described. He breaks through the fog of the senses by separating himself from his astral subjectivity. This is a quality of the individual self which is active within the blood. The human being now attains a state of conscious objectivity and realizes his oneness with the outer world, with the whole cosmos. He can now say: my individual self can grasp the essence of the tree, for my self is also objectively in the tree. This is an example for the relationship between the blood and the nerve systems.

The particular nature of the stigmata are also to be considered as belonging to this phenomenon of the transformation of the blood. For roughly seven months the wounds have remained virtually unchanged. They do not heal, neither however do they become inflamed. When a wound persists for such a long time it is usually always to be found in a state of inflammation, otherwise it would heal. However no inflammation has occurred and neither could any swelling of the lymph nodes be detected. The wounds bleed on some Fridays or in particular situations. Blood loss is mostly minimal.

Our observations indicate that the extent of the blood loss seems to match the individual constitution of the particular stigmatic. It has already been shown that the Mystery of Golgotha gave rise to the renewal of the phantom. From the incorruptible body of the Resurrected Christ something like a seed of the phantom body has been planted into every human being. It is now up to every individual person, by turning his soul and spirit to Christ, to nurture the development of this seed. Each seed of the phantom body originates from the one divine source and in its essential being belongs as a result to the divine, yet each one is individually created and has an individual character, just like an item of clothing to which the human adapts himself and with which he can be totally interwoven. Just as the individual selves of two people can never be identical, so can the phantom bodies of two individuals as well not be the same. This is the gift of the new covenant, the new world, which has been created for us only through Christ's Death and Resurrection. From now on the blood shall no longer be the bearer of the group soul, but the bearer of the individual self. Christ demonstrated this by uniting from the Cross Mary, His Mother, with His disciple John: 'Woman, behold, thy son!—Behold, thy mother!' Also when He says: 'Whoever does not leave their father, mother, brother and sister, cannot be my disciple' (Rudolf Steiner's paraphrase of Luke 14:26 in *Rosicrucian Wisdom* GA 99), it is to be understood in this way. The phantom body of an individual is therefore unique precisely because it emanates directly from Christ. One can therefore assume that a person with a lymphatic temperament, as for example Therese Neumann of Konnersreuth,★ tends to high blood loss and fluctuations in weight sooner than someone who is more athletic.

★ Therese Neumann (1898–1962) German Catholic mystic and stigmatic.

About Therese Neumann it is known that every Friday she lost large amounts of blood and lost up to seven pounds in weight. This shows particularly clearly how the transformed body can regenerate itself solely from its spiritual source, for she did not receive any blood transfusions. She had also regained the lost weight after three days at the latest despite not eating or drinking anything.

This again provides us with an example of the penetration of blood into another area of the body, namely the metabolism. Again the corresponding area is marked in diagram 3 (p.36).

The current state of knowledge of so-called scientists, which in general is firmly entrenched in our minds as well, teaches that blood is formed from substances which the human being receives via his food—like protein, sugar, iron. If the person receives insufficient amounts of these substances symptoms of deficiency appear. These can range from loss of energy to progressive wasting of muscle tissues, anaemia and to organ insufficiency.

All of these observations are correct in themselves when seen in an isolated sense—but they are not true. They are untrue because they have been made from a standpoint which provides no total overview of the nature of the human being. In his Christmas Imagination Rudolf Steiner characterized the normal scientist as a flea who chips out a tiny little piece from a human collarbone with his little hammer. The flea-scientist now uses the results of the investigation into this bone fragment to draw conclusions about the whole human organism (GA 229, 6 October 1923).

From its flea perspective present-day science has to deny such phenomena as the fact of someone living without food or drink. This must be pronounced a deception, as has also been the case with Kaspar Hauser. Those individuals who represent this science still owe us an answer to the question: what benefits could Kaspar Hauser have gained for himself by claiming to have lived for years on bread and water, by being unable to eat any meat or by succumbing to poisoning from smelling alcohol?

Anthroposophical spiritual science, however, is able to explain absolutely phenomena such as these, because it observes the inter-connections of the human organism from a higher viewpoint. It becomes clear to whoever looks at the world of the senses from the 'standpoint' of the spirit world that the human being is only able to sustain himself through the presence of the spiritual hierarchies and their active working within his physical body. The human in all his being is interpenetrated with the activity of divine beings. One learns to understand the line from the *Foundation Stone Meditation*: 'Man is from God'.

The differing perspectives can be illustrated by the example of the blood, which we have just been speaking about. From the perspective of spiritual science it must be said concerning blood that it is first of all the physical expression of the individual self in a physical human being. As a result, it goes without saying that from a point of view which provides a total overview of the human being, blood can only truly be blood when it is active in its proper sphere, namely, circulating within the human organism—engendering the individual selfhood of the person standing physically there in front of you. When a doctor takes a blood sample, whatever is said about this blood can only ever stem from the perspective of a flea. Fifty millilitres of individuality cannot be placed under a microscope.

Only when present-day science brings itself to search for the origin and continued existence of everything physical in the spirit will it be able to understand and recognize that it can be possible for a human being to continue living despite not eating or drinking anything.

On Maundy Thursday of this year I ate my last portion of physical food and from this moment on I have never felt the need to eat anything physical again. A quotation from Rudolf Steiner will clarify once again the relationship between nutrition and the phantom: 'One way of comprehending to some extent this degeneration is that from the beginning of human development this phantom was actually meant to remain untouched by the material elements absorbed as food by the human being from the mineral, plant and animal kingdoms. It was meant to remain untouched by these elements' (GA 131, 14 October 1911).

We can therefore ask ourselves the question, how can the body maintain itself without any physical food, what does the phantom live from?

We are reminded of the prayer that Jesus Christ Himself gave us, the Lord's Prayer: 'Give us this day our daily bread', is the usual translation. In his esoteric Lord's Prayer Rudolf Steiner characterizes this 'daily bread' as 'the food of the spirit, the bread of life' (GA 268). Here it is already apparent what kind of bread is involved. But even a superficial examination of the text of the prayer makes it clear that it is a question of spiritual nourishment. If you look at all the petitions one after the other it stands out that they are concerned with the condition of the human soul and spirit and with its development. It would be sheer absurdity to assume that a petition for a profane, well-laid lunch table would come between the petition that God's will be done and the petition for the forgiveness of sins. Continued bodily existence is in fact being prayed for, but through the means of spiritual nourishment, the bread of life. The accompanying word 'spiritual' is missing in the original Greek text but it is represented by the formulation 'Heaven and Earth' which underlies the Hebrew word *Malchut*. When the human being is in the flesh upon the Earth he is nourished as a spiritual being by the spirit. *Malchut* (the Kingdom) indicates this link between spiritual nourishment from Heaven and the incarnated human being on Earth. The people living at the time of Christ understood only or rather precisely *by means of* this formulation that with bread the Body of Christ was meant, as was also anticipated in the Last Supper. Through the Mystery of Golgotha, the body of the Earth became the Body of Christ, through the Resurrection the petition in the Lords's Prayer for 'nourishment of the spirit' was fulfilled.

Only a few hundred years later, in the so-called Vulgate, the original Latin text of the Lord's Prayer, it was obviously deemed necessary to add an unambiguous adjective to the *panem nostrum* to prevent it becoming understood in a secular way: *supersubstantialem* meaning 'Give us this day our *super-physical* bread'.

This adjective was again in turn lost a few hundred years later, this time by reason of the spiritual content of the words not being understood. Only at the present time is a new awareness for these things beginning to awaken.

It is therefore absolutely not the case that someone who is alive but outwardly not eating anything does not receive any form of nourishment. It is just that he does not nourish himself with physical food. Incidentally, the necessity of receiving spiritual nourishment applies to every single person. We are all dependent on this bread. You can observe in daily life what happens when someone denies the divine spiritual core of his being and devotes himself solely to the world of the senses. First the person becomes lethargic in his heart, takes no more interest in the lives of other people and develops a certain form of indifference. If this way of living also continues into the following incarnations, this will have serious consequences for the future development of the individual as well as for the development of the Earth. Instead of refinement, of becoming more spiritual, a hardening ensues. All these dismal consequences are described to us in the Apocalypse of John. There is only one antidote against this hardening. A sacrifice of love for another person is the basis for all good human development.

In the first lecture we went in detail into the different reasons with which we struggled through to the decision to hold these lectures to an internal audience. All this cannot be repeated now. However, there is something which lies heavily on my mind and that is a personal request I would like to repeat. With all the lectures and information being given please do not focus on my person but on that being who is acting through the phenomena. Please take me as a kind of 'object of study', though a holy reverence towards the Christ Being should be present. This is the only possibility for experiencing consciously the meeting of His Being and yours. Only when the most precious element of the soul of every single individual opens itself can the intellect withdraw into the background in favour of an awareness of the spirit. Whoever has the courage to look deep into his own soul, into his own abyss, will open his heart to Him—to Him and the mystery of His former, present and future epiphanies. From this innermost light, from the recovery of this light in our innermost holy places, arises the seed which will unite us with His Being. In order to represent this I will again use Rudolf Steiner's diagram which we are familiar with from Peter Tradowsky's contribution. I will add two arrows, however, the one indicating the replication of the one phantom body of Christ, while the other (broken line) refers to the return of a mankind transformed—through putting on the phantom—to Christ.

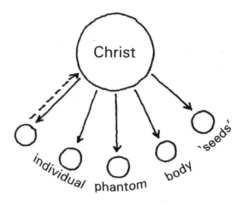

Diagram 4

In our present age we now have the gift of Anthroposophy available to us as an aid to knowledge. It is waiting to be put to use. It is time to start by abandoning simple belief and step by step to put in its place a living understanding gained by developing our knowledge. The question can be asked why belief should be replaced by a search for knowledge. Several religious people with whom I am friends are of the opinion you should not ask any questions, you should simply believe and then everything you need would be given to you. Understanding will be given as a gift after death.

The way I see it, this is inadequate. The age of the consciousness soul requires a new form of activity. The gift of the Resurrection is without doubt a gift that was given for all mankind. Paul expresses this when he says: 'Christ did not die only for the Jews, but also for the heathen' (Acts 26:23). If now mankind wants to respond to this gift, to use it for its future development—for that after all is what it was given for—it has to acquire an understanding for the Christ Being, for the spiritual interconnections of the Resurrection. It has to sharpen its awareness, and let its spirit shine. When at night the human being expands into the spheres of the planets and consciously looks with the eyes of the spirit into the sphere of the Sun, he is penetrated by a truth based on the laws of life: after earthly death the individual self creates from this sphere those forces it will need for the shaping of its future etheric body. However, obtaining these forces is dependant on the level of understanding the individual self in its life on Earth has developed concerning the Lord of the sphere of the Sun and concerning the gift of the Christ impulse. Generally, it is only possible to find a tree at a particular spot some day if previously a seed has been placed precisely at this spot in the Earth. The human being does indeed plant this seed in his life on Earth, but can find the place in the spiritual world again because true striving for knowledge always takes place in the sphere of the spirit and is written into it. In order therefore to find Christ in the sphere of the Sun I have to work at knowing Him in my life on Earth. Only when I know something, can I find it again. Only if I sow, can I harvest. It is therefore dangerous to wait until death before wanting to know, for in this way the human being will be lost in the spiritual world, without any orientation.

And precisely in respect of the phenomena described in this series of lectures, I am coming round more and more to speak *against* the presentation of them as sheer miracles, and more and more for the concrete 'application' of Anthroposophy. These phenomena provide precisely the impulse to work epistemologically and not just believe. Their apparent inexplicability prompts an anthroposophist to penetrate the phenomena with awareness, to use Anthroposophy as a tool. It seems as if the spiritual world has placed this phenomenon here in our anthroposophical circle in order to challenge us to become active in two areas which as a result of their complexity and significance we often shy away from:

1. Striving with heart and soul to gain an awareness of the secrets of the Mystery of Golgotha. Rudolf Steiner pointed out again and again that he could only give a part of the essential insights into this mystery and that the other part is to be a fruit of knowledge in the future.

2. Striving to gain insight into the organization of the human body, for this is the sphere of the highest spiritual beings of the hierarchies. The first hierarchy is active in the physical body—not in the etheric, not in the astral, but in the physical body and this is connected from the very beginning with the Christ Being. For this reason, in his fresco of the stigmatization of St Francis, Giotto painted the Christ Being as a six-winged cherub or seraph. This being acted upon the stigmatized body and transformed it right down into the blood which is able to generate itself from the superphysical bread and maintain the body through the spirit.

That this can happen within all of us is the warming trust the knowledge of Christ gives us every day.

Peter Tradowsky

It has already been mentioned that for Judith von Halle the stigmatization is accompanied by the experience of the time Christ lived, with the Christ event as it happened on the physical plane, historically and physically perceptible in the Easter Week, at Easter itself and beyond. This state of being back in the time of Christ is suffused, as I dare say everyone felt, with a sympathy and compassion filling the entire heart and soul. Present in addition is also the concern for a knowledge based on spiritual science, which we ourselves feel here committed to, and which has hopefully also become clear in what has already been presented. The spheres of experience linked to the karmic phenomenon of stigmatization meet abilities in perception in Judith von Halle which she brought with her into this incarnation.

Basically every person bears within himself everything he has acquired in all his incarnations and has brought to fruition in his life after death. Attention has already been drawn to this law of the development of the individual self through the Christ event on another occasion by means of a quotation from *Occult Science: An Outline*. Even when he brings the mature fruits of his own self-development into existence with him the human being is always aware that these fruits are at the same time a grace for which the deed on Golgotha and of the Resurrection are to be thanked.

Accompanying Judith von Halle along the path of her life since childhood is something which can best be expressed through words from Novalis, whom she values a great deal:

> The most arbitrary prejudice is to deny man the ability to be *outside* himself, to have an awareness beyond the senses. The human being is in the position to be an extrasensory being at any moment. Without this he would not be a citizen of the world, he would be an animal. Admittedly, sober-mindedness and self awareness in this state are very difficult as it is so constantly and so necessarily connected with the changes in our remaining states. The more, how-

ever, we are able to be aware of this state, the more alive, the stronger, the more sufficient is the conviction that arises; the belief in true revelations of the spirit. It is not looking, hearing, or feeling; it is composed of all three together, more than all three: a perception of direct certainty, a glimpse of my life at its most truest and most truly mine. Thoughts change into laws, wishes into their fulfilment. For the weak the fact of this moment is an article of faith (Blüthenstaub 23, in: *Novalis: Schriften*, Stuttgart, 2nd ed. 1960, p.420f.).

This awareness expressed in the words of Novalis has to a certain extent long been a characteristic of the sleeping and waking states of Judith von Halle. When asleep a certain continuity of consciousness, an awakening in an expanded state of consciousness in our spiritual cosmic home, is present in the way 'continuity of consciousness' is described by Rudolf Steiner in *Knowledge of the Higher Worlds*; when awake the possibility of an extended, conscious form of perception, imbued with thought, going beyond the things of the senses. This is certainly a very difficult subject to be speaking about, but it seems necessary in order to clarify the fact that the experiences connected with the stigmatization are only one aspect, the other aspect exists independently of the stigmatization through the abilities of perception and awareness mentioned. This aspect is visible in the spiritual scientific exploration of the experiences, and one is free to believe in its authenticity or not on the basis of the actual content.

Perhaps from this it can become clear why some judgements and claims which have come to our ears are untenable. It is said, for example, that stigmatization is 'atavistic'. By the term atavistic is understood an ancient form of perception of supersensible things bound to the body, a 'kind of clairvoyance of the fourth post-Atlantean period still resounding with the lingering echoes of a dream-like state' (GA 173, 24 December 1916) in which the self-awareness of the human being is not present. This can however hardly be claimed for someone who has acquired the just mentioned 'continuity of consciousness'. In this sense Francis of Assisi, generally recognized to be the first stigmatic and 'the first great materialist' according to Rudolf Steiner, as he was the first to strongly develop an 'eye for the earthly, a feeling for the earthly', can if anything be considered more as a 'forerunner' than as someone with atavistic characteristics. It is interesting that only towards the end of the Middle Ages, at the beginning of the Modern Age, a personality with stigmata first appeared and that precisely this first stigmatic was someone who introduced essential qualities of soul for the Modern Age, for the development of the consciousness soul, namely a 'feeling for matter' and a 'wonderful feeling for Nature'. Francis of Assisi was 'the first . . . among the great figures who completely turned their gaze away from everything originating from the ancient visionary, fantasy-filled way of life' (GA 292, 8 October 1916).

Another claim which is heard again and again and which is also levelled at other stigmatics is that stigmatization is a form of auto-suggestion. Apart from the fact that this claim is evidence of a lack of respect towards the fate of an individual person, it remains only to be said as a reminder that stigmatization is the living through of the events of the time of Christ, consciously and repeatedly, occurring under extreme physical, psychological and spiritual pain. Coming from individuals who have studied the concepts of spiritual science, the accusation of auto-suggestion is very questionable. Of course, the first question a person will often ask in the face of his karma is: why have I now been struck by fate? Looking deeper, however, a truth arises which Novalis has put into words: 'Everything that happens, I intend!' Here, of course, is not meant the everyday self nor the possibility of causing something like the stigmata, rather it points to the sphere of the real, the true self, which reveals itself in karma.

We hope that these lectures in their entirety will speak for them-selves and that it will become clear that the claims mentioned above have no basis in fact and that the prejudices the intellect only too quickly provides, especially in the face of such puzzling phenomena, are examined and tested seriously before being passed on to others.

II

THE STATIONS OF CHRIST'S PATH TO
SPIRIT MAN

The Mystery of Golgotha as the end of the old and beginning of the new initiation

12 December 2004

Peter Tradowsky

Dear Members, dear Friends,

For today's lecture on the new initiation which appeared in the awakening of Lazarus, it is important to take a spiritual law into account which is in this case, but also for much else in life and in karma, a decisive prerequisite for understanding. In physical existence we are used to a cause producing an effect—and for the physical world this is appropriate. Chronologically the cause precedes the effect and in the world of space and time this cannot be any other way. This law, however, is not valid in and for the spiritual world in this form. There it is absolutely possible that the effect appears before the cause. Without this insight it is impossible to understand how the Transfiguration on Mount Tabor, the awakening of Lazarus and the Last Supper can have happened, as they clearly presuppose the Resurrection of Christ at Easter, although seen chronologically this appeared only later.

Rudolf Steiner once formulated the spiritual law meant here with regard to karma in this way: 'With the earthly concept of time the human being believes that something happening here or there can have an effect only in relation to what follows afterwards. However, in the spiritual world it is so, that something happening reveals itself beforehand in its effects, that in its effects it is already present beforehand. Where does the blessing of karma come from? From what in our development on the Earth has this blessing that karma exists arisen? Karma comes from no other force in the whole of evolution than from Christ' (GA 107, 22 March 1909).

Judith von Halle

Dear Members, dear Friends,

In accordance with the title of our lecture we wish today to go into the different ways of initiation by focusing mainly on several significant aspects of the Mystery of Golgotha.

In the further course of the lecture I will be supplementing the observations from the perspective of spiritual science with a few details I have acquired by means of my living through the events at the time of Christ.

The pre-Christian initiation was based on an intensive preparatory phase of the neophyte. This first of all created the preconditions for the actual initiation through the purification over months and years at the side of the occult teacher of the neophyte's astral desires and habits. It was not just anybody who could become a neophyte. A certain mixture of the blood was necessary; the neophyte had to possess the gift of clairvoyance inherited through the bloodline. For this reason there always existed in pre-Christian mystery cults one or more castes of priests, whose progeny stood under strict ritual observation.

The process of initiation was eventually begun with a 'drink of forgetfulness' which dampened awareness and put the neophyte into a sleep-like state for three-and-a-half days. Under these conditions not only did the individual self and the astral body separate from the physical body but also a large part of the etheric body. During this time the neophyte wandered through the astral and devachanic worlds and was permitted to see and experience those things he had before only learned about. He saw the Logos, though the activity of the Logos could only be experienced as far as the etheric body as a result of the dampening of awareness and the sleep or death-like state. In this respect ancient initiation did anticipate to a certain extent what the incarnation of the Logos was to enable for all mankind, but its influence did not reach into the physical body.

During this entire process the neophyte was in the care of and dependent on the teacher who finally brought him back into physical consciousness as an initiate. He was now a witness to the spiritual world and the world of the gods spoke through him to the people. In this way he became the spiritual leader of a people or of a tribe, a leader of others who were not yet able to share in his spiritual knowledge.

In order to clarify the difference between the origins of the ancient and the new initiations it is helpful to take a look at the evolution of mankind from a certain perspective: before man stood upon the Earth as a being of flesh and blood, in a form which we today would call human, his higher being existed outside of him, united with other beings in a divine totality. Rudolf Steiner describes the form in which the human being appears in the Lemurian period as a kind of vessel which was preparing itself to be filled at a certain point in time with its higher being. But how did this come about?

When the Earth was still united with the Sun, the Elohim—the name given to them in Genesis—the Exousiai, the Spirits of Form, were living there. They endowed mankind with the warmth of the blood. This moment was the first in which the human being had a feeling of self in relation to his body of warmth. When the Sun finally separated from the Earth the Elohim went with it and following a phase of solidification and separating out of the Moon, they left one Elohim behind on the Moon in direct proximity to the Earth. His brothers on the Sun were reflected in Him, so that the human being, in the time which followed, could come into contact with the Sun Logos via this Moon god. This Elohim is called 'Y H W H'—Yahveh—in the Bible. It was Yahveh who breathed the divine breath into Man. He is also characterized in the Torah as a wind god, for the spirit body of this god is the air, which can penetrate into the human being via the warmth of his blood. The ability to breathe, and also as a result language, were developed in this way, with the possibility one day for the human being also to be able to pronounce the word 'I'.

We can now set out the evolution of mankind in the following sequence of stages:

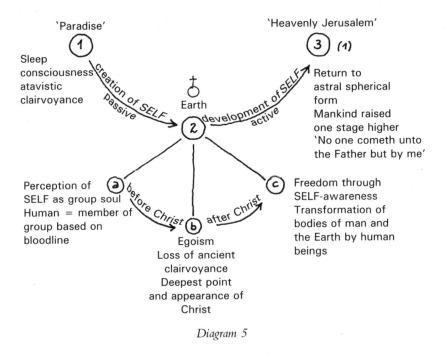

Diagram 5

At the beginning of his evolution on the Earth the human being was one with the divine, though he only possessed something like a dream consciousness and as a result atavistic clairvoyance, as his higher being existed outside of his body. It is apparent that the ritual ceremonies in pre-Christian initiation sought to imitate this condition by the neophyte having to 'forget' his normal consciousness, his higher being existing at the same time outside of his body.

Rudolf Steiner compares the condition of mankind before it incarnated into a body of flesh with a glass filled with water (cf. for example GA 96, 25 March 1907). One could indeed imagine the liquid consisting of thousands of single drops but in the glass they all form together one homogenous liquid and are not separate from one another (see diagram 5, stage 1).

Through the Fall, the luciferic temptation, Mankind sank down into the physical denseness of the Earth and by and large assumed its present visible bodily form. A slow process of individualization began at this point. You must not imagine this individualization as something happening in the same way as today. Taking the analogy of the glass of water, you could say the glass gets tipped over and the liquid runs out.

There do not suddenly exist thousands of individual drops, rather, larger islands of water form due to surface tension. This clustering together represents the bloodline. In the time before Christ love as well was somewhat different from what it is today. Love only occurred between members of the same ethnic group. In this way it is understandable when it says in the Bible: so and so was 300 years old. Even at that time humans obviously did not reach this 'Biblical age'. What is meant is the spirit of the corresponding personality, which remained, as well as its experiences, in the memory of the descendants, as the self was totally tied up with the blood flowing through the line of inheritance. A relic from this time is the formation of cases in the Hebrew language. The first person singular, the 'I' form, does not exist in the declinated form. Even liturgical texts always speak in the first person plural. The 'I' form is reserved till the present-day solely for God. The *eyeh asher eyeh—I am the I am*—applied *to Yahveh,* who likewise evolved. He changed more and more from a wind god to an Earth god, in order to prepare for the appearance of Christ on the Earth. The only ones however standing in contact with Yahveh were the individual initiates who acted as the awareness of their brothers in the group soul. (See diagram 5, stage 2a. The Earth stage in the diagram is divided into three parts—2a, 2b, 2c—and is intended to indicate the period before the Mystery of Golgotha as well as the time during Christ's presence on the Earth and the period of evolution of the Earth after Christ.) The gradual breaking down of this law of the blood was ultimately an expression of the process of progressive individualization. This can be illustrated using the image of the glass of water: more and more small islands of water are formed, more and more smaller interconnections, which take on more the form of drops (cf. GA 96, 1 April 1907). Nations of one blood turned into tribes, then families and so on. But this process of individualization was luciferic. Rudolf Steiner says that the blood became egoistic (cf. GA 96, 25 March 1907). The Fall onto the physical Earth was an absolutely positive step for mankind as it initiated the development of the individual self; at the same time, however, the 'phantom' was destroyed, which exposed humans to the influence of Lucifer. As this development continued, access to knowledge of the spiritual worlds dried up, ancient clairvoyance declined. At this time of the most spiritual darkness 'the cosmic light of spirit entered the earthly flow of Being' (*The Foundation Stone Meditation*) in order to restore the marred archetypal image of the human being. Only in this way, through the sacrifice of the Sun-Logos, could the human individual self become free and truly independent. The victory of the spirit over matter and death, which in former times was only perceptible to the inner vision of the initiates, now became capable of being seen and experienced by all mankind. Christ brought a new wisdom into the world. It was new to the extent that it came as a universal truth, which every single human being, without exception, could develop within himself. This wisdom founded a new covenant of love: by relating towards one another in a totally different form no longer based on the blood, humans can, from now on, experience love through the power of the heart, through a spiritual bond. In this way can the words spoken by Christ on the Cross to Mary and John be understood: 'Woman, behold, thy son! [...] Behold, thy mother!' (John 19:25–27). Here in the last act of God while living in a human body, and simultaneously the first act of His sacrifice, this covenant is founded by uniting two people together who are not connected by blood through the spirit and in the name of Him who has made this new way of life possible. Christ is the unifying force. This also comes to expression in His words: 'Whoever does not leave father, mother, brother, sister cannot be my disciple' (Rudolf Steiner's paraphrase of Luke 14:26 in *Rosicrucian Wisdom* GA 99).

At the moment of the appearance of Christ and ultimately of the sacrifice of Christ, through which He unites Himself with the Earth, at the moment of descent into the depths of matter, the Earth itself becomes the Kingdom of God, becomes the tenth Sephiroth of the Tree of Sephiroth, becomes *Malchut* (see diagram 5, stage 2b, p. 56).

The subsequent evolution (or potential evolution) of mankind is based on the individual self in every single person, transformed and awakened by Christ, being able to spiritualize his physical and supersensible bodies. Mankind has, so to speak, walked through the deepest valley (in diagram 5, stage number 2, p.56) and can now, if it wants, take the path back to its origins, to its home in the spiritual world. This is of course something totally new for humans (this could be designated in the diagram by the number 3, the third evolutionary stage), for one day they will be entering this world as transformed individuals, able *consciously* to perceive the spiritual world.

Christ created a replacement for the pre-Christian ties of family which were severed by the process of individualization: the act of 'putting on the phantom'. We recall to mind the image already used from Rudolf Steiner in the lecture cycle *From Jesus to Christ* (GA 131):

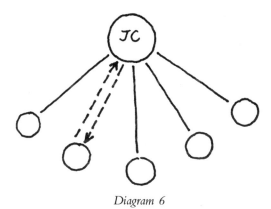

Diagram 6

From the archetype, the Resurrection body of Christ, seeds of the phantom body (arrow pointing down) emanate to every single human being. The human being can bring these to flower himself by working with the new possibilities open to him towards perceiving the spirit, towards spiritualizing himself. Through the work and activity of the self the human being can develop a relationship to the Christ phantom (arrow pointing up). This generates the new brotherhood of love, the new spiritual family bond. (see diagram 5, stage 2c, p. 56).

The differences of the new initiation and the pre-Christian initiation are now evident. Through the penetration of the Logos down into the last fibre of the physical body, His influence could become directly experienced in the human being. In this way Christ can be experienced in the depths of the physical body, not just as far as the etheric body as it was in the period before Christ. This can only happen because the human being no longer dampens his awareness but, on the contrary, retains it, even sharpens it. Thinking, a clear understanding, is the first step in initiation. For this reason an initiator, at least a human one, is no longer necessary. The truth flows directly from Christ into those individuals who through their work on developing the self become aware of the truth. As a result the self becomes completely un-egoistic. Rudolf Steiner says in his lecture cycle GA 96 (25 March 1907):

> They [human beings] have not yet found a way of connecting with this universal wisdom. Humans will find this connection as a result of truly starting to work with this universal wisdom and making it as strongly individual as possible. [...] When you have realized that for universal wisdom no particular standpoint exists, that holding any particular view means nothing other than that you have not yet developed far enough, only then can you understand the idea of the Holy Spirit. Only those who have not reached perfection have points of view. Those individuals who are nearing the spirit of truth have no standpoint. They know they have to devote themselves selflessly to the primal universal wisdom.

Humans themselves can now through the Christian, through the Rosicrucian initiation, through present-day spiritual science—which Rudolf Steiner also calls a science of the Grail—become preparers of the 'Heavenly', the 'New Jerusalem'; in other words, they can transform the body of the Earth into a spiritualized body, into the Sun.

In the diagram you can now recognize that up to the Mystery of Golgotha the evolution of mankind follows a more passive path. At the beginning of his evolution on the Earth the human being is united with God and directed by Him. He receives the foundation for his life and development through the influences of higher spiritual beings. Since the Mystery of Golgotha the human being is an independent, free being—which of course also brings great dangers with it—a being who has to become active in order to 'put on' the phantom, or has also the freedom not to do so.

The Mystery of Golgotha is the turning-point in the evolution of the Earth, in the evolution of mankind. Starting from this point, through the connection with the Christ Being, humans can return in a new way to the origin (to stage 1 or to stage 3 in our diagram): 'No one cometh unto the Father, but by me!' (John 14:6, see diagram 5, stage 3, p. 56)

Now how does this all-encompassing transformation through the sacrifice of Christ manifest itself? Christ inaugurates his Mysteries

Himself and in fact before His death, which constitutes the actual Mystery. In this way Christ reveals in advance several crucial basic elements of His new Mysteries, in order to facilitate a better understanding of the coming event for those who were around Him and with Him, thus manifesting the law of 'the effect *preceding* the cause', which for our earthly understanding appears to be a paradox. In addition to the details given by Rudolf Steiner it can be added that this law is not in any way a paradox from the perspective of the spiritual world. In the spiritual world the laws of space and time do not hold. The spiritual world is distinguished precisely through its spacelessness, through timelessness. But now this property of the spiritual world descends down to the Earth with the Christ Being, breaking in the process the purely physical, material laws. Nor is the phantom body subject to any physical or material bonds. It can free itself from them. As a result, the events on the road to Emmaus no longer remain an inexplicable wonder. The Resurrection body, the spiritual archetype of the human being, that Rudolf Steiner also called 'a real thought existing in the outer world' (GA 131, 10 October 1911) can reveal itself at different locations, at different times and in different forms and is not bound to the physical body. Three examples will be given which indicate an advance effect of the Mystery. They were all given to mankind at the time Christ was still living on the Earth and all are concerned with the future evolution of the human individual self.

The first example is a very profound one as it anticipates the glorification of the self through the Resurrection of Christ; it is the Awakening of Lazarus. In the Bible it is written about Lazarus that he had been dead for four days. This is a clear reference to something happening which goes beyond the ancient, pre-Christian initiation of three-and-a-half days. Christ receives news of the serious illness of Lazarus, but nevertheless waits another two days before returning to Bethany. At this point Lazarus is already dead. From my own experience of this Awakening I can say that Lazarus must have been dead for a longer time, as his family had left him, contrary to the funeral rites of the time, laid out in the house for quite a long time in the hope Jesus, Aramaic *Eashoa*, would come in the next few hours to awaken him—which however was not the case. Only when he had been lying there for at least one to two days was he prepared for the funeral and laid in the large family grave. There he lay for the time mentioned of roughly four days, before the wonder of the Awakening took place. Christ says however: 'This sickness is *not* unto death' (John 11:4). It was not to lead to the old death but to a resurrection. Lazarus was the rich young man we are familiar with from the Gospels, who one day asked Christ how he could attain immortal life (Matthew 19:20–22). After receiving the reply that he should keep the Commandments, and affirming that he did, he asked again what he was lacking for eternal life. Christ replied that Lazarus should part from his belongings and distribute them to the poor. But he did not do this. When Lazarus became ill and died this materialistic part of him fell away. He became through the Awakening, through the new Christian initiation, a new man who had to lay this part aside.

As we know from Rudolf Steiner Lazarus is a special figure (GA 265). He is the reincarnation of Hiram, the great master builder who erected the Temple of Solomon; he is the highest perfection of the line of Cain and had developed every member of his being up to the intellectual soul. The process of initiation through Christ united this Cain soul with the representative of the cosmic human, of the line of Abel, who at this time was already in the spiritual world, with John the Baptist. John the Baptist had been the reincarnation of Elias and was one stage ahead of the evolution of the rest of mankind; he was the 'voice in the wilderness', a voice in solitude, which is a reference to the already developed consciousness soul. In the process of the Awakening these two principles of mankind united and there emerged an individual who was the bearer of all the bodies (physical and supersensible) of the human being: the lower ones from the line of Cain, the upper ones as far as Atman, the Spirit Man, from the line of Abel. The awakened Lazarus-John bears alongside his physical body the Resurrection body, the phantom, developed through the power of Christ, and consequently represents the ideal of the future human being whom mankind shall take as a paradigm for its development. Lazarus-John became even before the Resurrection of Christ that being each individual human in the future can become through putting on the phantom himself. So that this could be understood and serve as a preparation for the events of Good Friday and Easter Sunday, the awakening of Lazarus occurred before the eyes of a large crowd and

NOTES

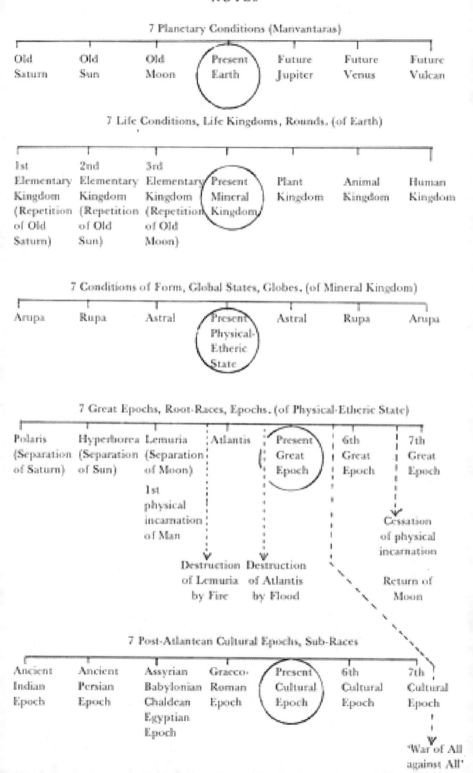

7 Planetary Conditions (Manvantaras)

| Old Saturn | Old Sun | Old Moon | Present Earth | Future Jupiter | Future Venus | Future Vulcan |

7 Life Conditions, Life Kingdoms, Rounds, (of Earth)

1st Elementary Kingdom (Repetition of Old Saturn) — 2nd Elementary Kingdom (Repetition of Old Sun) — 3rd Elementary Kingdom (Repetition of Old Moon) — Present Mineral Kingdom — Plant Kingdom — Animal Kingdom — Human Kingdom

7 Conditions of Form, Global States, Globes, (of Mineral Kingdom)

Arupa — Rupa — Astral — Present Physical-Etheric State — Astral — Rupa — Arupa

7 Great Epochs, Root-Races, Epochs, (of Physical-Etheric State)

Polaris (Separation of Saturn) — Hyperborea (Separation of Sun) — Lemuria (Separation of Moon) 1st physical incarnation of Man — Atlantis — Present Great Epoch — 6th Great Epoch — 7th Great Epoch

Destruction of Lemuria by Fire

Destruction of Atlantis by Flood

Cessation of physical incarnation

Return of Moon

7 Post-Atlantean Cultural Epochs, Sub-Races

Ancient Indian Epoch — Ancient Persian Epoch — Assyrian Babylonian Chaldean Egyptian Epoch — Graeco-Roman Epoch — Present Cultural Epoch — 6th Cultural Epoch — 7th Cultural Epoch

'War of All against All'

not amidst a quiet, small circle of people. This happened 'because of the multitude which standeth around . . . that they may believe . . .' as it is written in the Gospel (John 11:42).

A second example of an effect before the actual mystery event is the prayer Christ Himself gave his disciples, the Lord's Prayer. The Lord's Prayer was also given to mankind through Christ before its actual cause occurred. It describes the possibilities of development of man through the bond which unites him with Christ and through the knowledge arising from the work of the self. Rudolf Steiner represents this in a diagram within his lecture cycle GA 96 (28 January 1907):

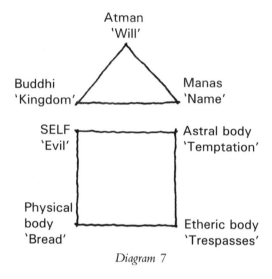

Diagram 7

On the basis of this diagram it is evident that the upper triangle can only arise through the active presence and relationship of the self to the three lower bodies. Through the Mystery of Golgotha the human being is able to develop these higher principles of his being. This is the task of the present and the future.

The third example for the law of the effect preceeding the cause is the Last Supper, which is actually the 'First' Supper. Here the body of the Earth is celebrated as the body of Christ before Christ descended— through His death on the Cross—into the ultimate depths of matter; before the irrevocable transformation of the Earth's aura. The body of Christ is the Earth, the bread, made from substances the Earth produces. The blood of Christ is the wine, the plant sap rising out of the

Earth. Through the Communion the human being receives the body and the blood of Christ. The transubstantiation is only possible through Christ's sacrifice of love, through the self freed from egoism, through a new selfless love independent of the bloodline. For this reason after this ceremonial act, in other words on the evening before His death, Christ speaks the words: 'Now is the Son of Man glorified and God is glorified in him. [...] A new commandment I give unto you, that ye love one another; even as I have loved you' (John 13:31–34).

These words shall provide the transition to the events of the Mystery itself, to the events of the Crucifixion. Here the realization begins of the content of the Mystery which Christ in the acts mentioned above made visible or prefigured. Through the penetration into the physical world of the Earth, through taking on a physical body, the sacrifice of love transforming the Earth and mankind was enacted. For this was an act which was done for mankind out of pure love and in itself was not necessary for the evolution of the Godhead. After the Baptism the Christ Being walked for three years on the Earth in the body of the Nathan Jesus. During this time the divine being penetrated more and more into physical matter—Christ experienced true humanity more and more in His being. He became more human. Consequently, to free mankind from its subjection to Lucifer (*Christus verus Luciferus* cf. for example GA 105, 10 August 1908) Christ descended into the depths of matter, at first into the body of Jesus in which He was ultimately tortured and crucified and then into the body of the Earth itself. As this resulted in a profound transformation of all matter—of the configuration as well of Man's being—it is of great significance *how* Christ penetrated into the very last fibre of the physical body. At the beginning it was shown how the human being in his past evolution, through the development of his blood and breathing, came to an initial 'awareness' of his self, his individuality. Precisely these two decisive physical features, which are totally interwoven with the activity of the self, were in turn through the sacrifice of Christ worked on, transformed and spiritualized through and through. And so I would like to ask you to share in the events of the Crucifixion which are shown to me every Friday. In advance I would like to say that it is not possible to speak of these things without triggering an (often uncomfortable) emotional response in the listeners, even when speaking about them in the most neutral manner possible. Not one person who in truth is able to call himself a Christian would refuse feeling sympathy for the fate, for the sacrifice of his Redeemer. The scale of Christ's suffering is anyway immeasurable, and cannot be put into words as He was not accustomed to experiencing physical and material pain. For the Sun Logos had never incarnated before. Here we will provide 'only' those details which are necessary for presenting a picture in line with the title of this lecture.

Christ was not just nailed to the Cross but also tied. Both processes have a deep mystical significance and are linked with the entry of the self through the blood and the breathing described above (cf. the second verse of *The Foundation Stone Meditation*: 'You live in the rhythm of heart and lungs [. . .] For the will of Christ is all around'). Before the nails were hammered into the hands and feet and the Cross erected, Christ was tied to the wood with cords. Apparently this was the way it was always done to prevent the tearing of the wounds by the nails. To take the weight, and in order to extend the time of suffering, three notches were hewn into the main post at the head, buttocks and feet. In addition, a board was attached for standing on. The Cross was first assembled on the spot, measuring it to fit Christ by marking in advance the positions for the nails on to the wood. The horizontal beams were not completely horizontal to the vertical beam, but were slotted into the ready-made holes in the side of the central beam like a Y. It became apparent however, after nailing the right hand on, that the palm of the left hand of the Redeemer did not reach over to the pre-drilled hole. To avoid the trouble of drilling another hole, however, a cord was tied around Christ's left wrist and pulled on with such tremendous force that His arm was dislocated and as a consequence it was possible to hammer a nail into the predrilled hole. The upper part of the body was in this way stretched to its limit, as a result of which He automatically drew His knees up. In order now to be able to nail the feet at the predrilled spot He was bound tightly at the hips, and the knees were likewise bound down. Through the legs being pulled down the chest arched forwards in a position of most unspeakable tension away from the Cross. Christ therefore did not hang in the form of a Y on a T-shaped cross as art and tradition have made popular, but quite the contrary: He Himself formed, through the extreme tension of His body bound to the Y-shaped wooden cross, the horizontal T-Cross. These measures caused Christ to die, not from the nails, not from the resulting bleeding, but from suffocation. The nails caused severe bleeding. From Rudolf Steiner we find explained that in this mystical process the 'egoistic blood' of mankind flowed out in exactly the right amount that was necessary. In the same way that the materialistic part of Lazarus had to die and leave his body as a symbol of the future and as an actual process belonging to the Mysteries, so on the Cross did the luciferic, egoistic blood of mankind flow vicariously from Jesus Christ's wounds.

At the same time a second Mystery process occurred relating to the transformation of the organ of breathing. The longer Christ hung on the Cross bound and tied in this extreme form the more onerous each breath became. The breath penetrated in this way deeper and deeper into the physical body. Doctor Lothar Vogel describes the breathing at the moment of death: 'It is again the astral forces which deepen the inhalation one-sidedly as death approaches. This breathing type leads ultimately to strong, single inhalations. The astral forces sink deeper and deeper into the body, until ultimately they completely displace the etheric and in one last deep inhalation draw life to a close. (From: *Der dreigliedrige Mensch*, Dornach, 4th rev. ed. 2005, p.303.) You can imagine how much more strongly this process occurs when someone experiences suffocation.

In death the power of Christ could reach ultimately into the kingdom of Ahriman, laying his forces in chains in the 'Descent into Hell' between Good Friday and Easter Sunday. 'Ahriman had the power to impose on Christ the necessity of truly uniting Himself with the Earth, [...] of leading Christ to death. And through death the Christ Being merged with the being of the Earth' (GA 148, 18 November 1913).

The words of the cry '*Eli, Eli, lama sabachtani!*', which have been conveyed to us, clearly indicate that in His respiratory distress, in the transformation and new configuration of the process of breathing, Christ turns to the Elohim. In fact Christ calls 'Eloi, Eloi ...' which means: Elohim, Elohim.

In the various translations of the Bible two different interpretations emerge. In the Luther translation Psalm 22 is quoted; the words 'My God, my God, why hast thou forsaken me?' (Matthew 27:46) are rendered namely in the original Hebrew: '*Eli, Eli, lama asawtani?*' In Hebrew the verb *azav* means 'to forsake'. Hence the variation in form to *zabach* which in Hebrew means 'to sacrifice'.

Nowadays it is known that Christ mainly spoke Aramaic. And so Emil Bock, Menge and Zwingli have the words: '*Eli, Eli, lama sabachtani!*'

What however is actually meant by these words? 'My God, my God, why hast thou forsaken me?' They are almost the last words of Christ. How could God forsake Him at the moment of fulfilment of His mission?

We are familiar from Rudolf Steiner with a further meaning of the cry: '*Eli, Eli, lama sabachtani!*' He gives these words the meaning 'My God, my God, how thou hast raised me/how thou hast glorified me!' or 'My God, my God, how you have revealed the self!' (GA 96, 1 April 1907). This interpretation is of fundamental importance as it describes the decisive moment for the future development of man, the moment at which he becomes a free being. Only through this Mystery event has the development of our world as we know it today—even the development of Anthroposophy—been at all possible. But how is this translation compatible with the Aramaic? Both meanings are totally different and supposedly contradictory. They are indeed different but not contradictory.

From my experience of the events of the Passion from roughly two thousand years ago I would like to try and point out a certain ambiguity with which Christ often spoke to humans. But even without this authentic experience many indications of this kind of ambiguity are to be found. Jesus Christ was deeply connected with the Hebraic culture. He carried within Himself all the wisdom of the religion of His people. Rudolf Steiner explains this phenomenon by means of the wisdom of the Solomon Jesus child who united with the being of the Nathan Jesus. The genealogy itself found in the Bible shows that the body of Jesus into which Christ Himself could ultimately enter was the culmination of thousands of years of preparation of the bloodline.

A description has already been given at the beginning of the lecture of how the wisdom of the forefathers was passed on through the bloodline to the next generation. The body of *Eashoa* carried within itself all the memories of the leaders of the Hebrew people. *Eashoa* was familiar with the Scriptures; all the prophecies were after all related to His coming. It was also a self-evident part of life at the time that the people lived with and for the meaning of these words of the prophets. That is why *Eashoa* often used the words from the Scriptures in His teaching sessions, changing them, however, and filling them with an entirely new meaning so that to the disciples it often seemed as though they had never heard these words before. It was in fact as though the actual familiar ritual words were transformed, for Christ had created with His appearance on the Earth the new covenant, had caused a turning-point in the evolution of mankind. The words received a new meaning. There lay a meaning for the *future* in them, which was unknown up until then (and for the most part up until the present day). 'He interpreted to them in all the scriptures' is how it is written in the Gospels (Luke 24:27). *His* manner of interpreting the Scriptures was indeed unique. As these interpretations were constantly relating to the future development of mankind, the disciples understood, with the exception of Lazarus-John, at first very little. The reason for this lay in the fact that the consciousness soul had not been developed yet and in the fact that only after the completion of the Mystery of Golgotha did a higher meaning for some of these interpretations and deeds of Christ arise for them. Only at Whitsun, with the pouring out of the spirit, did the doors of understanding open in the hearts and minds of the disciples.

We find one example of the ambiguity between traditional ritual and a renewed meaning for the future in the Festival of the *Pesach* sacrifice on Maundy Thursday. On this occasion a lamb would traditionally be slaughtered to venerate God. Christ Himself dispensed it among His disciples. Each one received from Christ his individual share handed out to him. This mystical gesture expresses what we have already heard about the Grail feast in *Parsifal* by Wolfram von Eschenbach. Every one receives exactly the food he craves. If we now bring to mind the details concerning the seeds of the phantom body emanating from Christ (see diagram 5, p. 56), it will be understandable that the decisive factor lies in the process of individualization, in the raising of the self, for each person develops his relationship to Christ in a highly individual way, and precisely this individual approach to Christ unites him with his brothers in spirit.

Christ offered the sacrifice of the *Pesach* as the rites prescribed. But in this mystical act lay the prefiguring of His own sacrificial death. What was new in this Maundy Thursday meal was therefore that not only a human sacrificed to God, but that God sacrificed Himself for mankind. It can be seen on the basis of this example what is meant by the above mentioned ambiguity.

Christ's last words can also be comprehended in this sense. Rudolf Steiner, with his translation of the above words, is pointing to the fundamental event for the evolution of mankind, the birth of the conscious and free self.

However, it cannot be denied that the translation of '*Eli, Eli, lama sabachtani*' actually is 'My God, my God, why hast thou forsaken me?' Now I would like to relate to you what I hear anew every Friday from out of His mouth. It is the words: '*Eloi, Eloi, l'ma shevachtani!*'—*shevach* means translated: 'improvement', and 'increase in value'. Again Christ uses words resembling Holy Scripture—here Psalm 22 with its *sabachtani*.

In Hebrew the alphabet consists exclusively of consonants, which at the same time stand for a particular numerical value. The vowels, especially in the past, were considered to be the divine breath, which was blown into the consonants and only through them could the word come alive. This immediately calls to mind the prologue of John's Gospel, in which the traditional holiness of the Word experienced in ancient Jewish culture comes to expression. The true Word is only formed through man's ability to breathe and speak. For this reason at that time, and this still applies at present to Holy Scripture, the vowels are left out of all words. As the understanding for this mystery disappeared in the time after Christ in favour of other developments, the writing of vowels above and below the consonants in the form of points and lines began in secular literature, in order to prevent any misunderstanding. Just suppose the English language likewise had at its disposal exclusively consonantal characters; then if you wanted to write the word 'mound' only the M, the N and the D would remain: MND. Now if there was someone wanting to read this word who had not heard it before or did not know the context, he could just as well form from these consonants put together in this way the words 'MiND', 'MoNaD' or 'MeND'. The word 'mound', consequently, would not be clearly recognizable.

Now something similar has occurred with the words *sabachtani* and *shevachtani*. The meaning of the words was handed down one-sidedly. For when you write down both versions the result is the following (reading from right to left):

'	נ	ת	ח	ב	ש		'	נ	ת	ח	ב	ש
(J)	N	T	CH	B	S		(J)	N	T	CH	V	SH

(J = replacement character for i)

Two words with converse meanings but spelt identically (in Hebrew). Only if you write in the vowel marks (found under the letters) and the additional characters (found in and above the letters) do you see what otherwise can only be heard:

'thou hast forsaken me'

(J)	N	T	CH	B	S
'	נ	תַ	ח	בַ	שֲ
i		a		a	a

'thou hast raised me'

(J)	N	T	CH	V	SH
'	נ	תַ	ח	בַ	שֶ
i		a		a	e

ש = s
שׁ = sh
ב = b
בֿ = w

Rudolf Steiner had heard the two meanings of the words on the Cross in the Akashic Chronicle and translated them for us. But apparently he did not hear the spoken Aramaic and allocated therefore the familiar and common words, '*Eli, Eli, lama sabachtani!*' to his second 'spiritual' translation as well: 'My God, my God, how thou hast raised me!'

The above mentioned ambiguity in the words of Jesus Christ has here a special reason as both meanings were cried out so to speak. This reason is to be found in the unique being of Christ Jesus, in the very being of Jesus and in the very being of Christ, which were in one and the same person.

The dying body of Jesus, whose higher being no longer remains bound to it in death, as it is free of the body and can ascend into the spirit, calls in its extreme distress: '*Eloi, Eloi, lama sabachtani?*'—'My God, my God, why hast thou forsaken me?'—'My God, my God, why hast thou, why hast my divine higher being forsaken me?' This body does not know the state of being forsaken by the indwelling divine core of its being (in accordance with the 22nd Psalm).

Christ, however, is preparing Himself for birth at the death of the body of Jesus. This is the interpretation Rudolf Steiner applies in his lectures *The Fifth Gospel* (GA 148). Here he describes the baptism, the entry of the Christ Being into the body of Jesus, as the conception, and the death of the body of Jesus as the birth of Christ: 'To a certain extent the Christ Being went through an embryonic stage of life from the baptism by John to the Mystery of Golgotha. The Mystery of Golgotha itself we have to understand as the earthly birth, in other words, the death of Jesus as the earthly birth of Christ. And we need to look for His actual earthly life *after* the Mystery of Golgotha' (GA 148, 3 October 1913).

In the *Study of Man* (GA 293) Rudolf Steiner refers to the moment of earthly death which opens for the first time, also for a normal person, the doors of knowledge: 'For reality is not in the surroundings, nor is it in appearances, rather it is the case that reality only gradually emerges by finding our way into this reality, so that reality only confronts us at the end. Basically, true reality would be what the human being sees at the moment when he can no longer express himself, namely at that moment as he passes through the gates of death' (GA 293, 26 August 1919). And so, in the face of the death of His bodily sheath, in the face of the fulfilment of His divine sacrifice, by which He purifies the blood and establishes the freedom of consciousness, the new, independent self, Christ calls out the words: '*Eloi, Eloi, l'ma shevachtani!*'—'My God, my God, how thou hast raised me!': 'My God, my God, how thou hast raised the Self in *Malchut*!' (the 'Kingdom' which is meant in the Lord's Prayer). This is the 'birth of the new world' (according to the fifth hymn from the *Hymns to the Night* by Novalis).

Only through this transformation of the human self by the power of the mysteries is the path of human evolution to the 'New Jerusalem' at all possible. If we consult once more diagram 5, p. 56, we can say that the step from the second to the new first (or third) stage of evolution can only be taken by means of this sacrifice. We have to thank Christ as a result for our freedom. Rudolf Steiner expressly points this out to us. His sacrifice of love, namely in becoming God in the Earth sphere of mankind by being born in the Earth as the Christ Sun through dying into the body of Jesus, is described by Novalis in the fifth hymn from his *Hymns to the Night*:

Eternal life was manifested in death,
You are death and make us truly whole.

The significance of the Mystery of Golgotha is so powerful and so profound that Rudolf Steiner spoke with justification of a 'Mystery'. Much at present still remains hidden from us. Only at the end of the Earth period, at the beginning of the Jupiter period, will the human being be able to grasp the Mystery of the Son in its complexity, in its divine grandeur and glory and in its divine splendour. Yet we shall continue step by step in our struggle for knowledge, Anthroposophy serving as our spiritual tool. We are all in the fortunate position of being able to make use of the possibilities Anthroposophy gives us for gaining knowledge. Each one of us can and should undertake research in a totally individual way, not speculating but researching in the spirit of Anthroposophy. The human being is called upon—for his own good and that of his brother—to sharpen his mind in the spirit of Michael, and to use and apply his mind so that the Son of God's gift to him of love and freedom does not have to remain in darkness.

An account of the events between Death and Resurrection (The Descent into Hell)

30 January 2005

Dear Members and Friends!

In the last lecture we looked at the development of the human self in pre-Christian times. And we focused on the impulse which gave mankind freedom and manifested itself in the dying of Jesus Christ on the Cross, through which the human self was saved from its inevitable descent into egoism. We discussed how, in the evolution of mankind before Christ, the first awakening of the human self, which was initiated by the Elohim, was connected with the blood and the breathing. What happened on the Cross again clearly showed the connection of the blood and the breathing with the transformation of the human self, which ultimately came to expression in the cry of Christ recorded in the Gospels with the words: *'Eli, Eli, lama sabachtani'*. The actual Aramaic wording of this cry was quoted, namely *'Eloi, Eloi, l'ma shevachtani!'* from which follows that precisely those Elohim were called on whose leader is Christ. We referred then to the two differing spiritual translations of this sentence by Rudolf Steiner from out of the Akashic Chronicle of which one points to the above mentioned transformation of the human self: 'My God, my God, how thou hast raised me!'—'My God, my God, how thou hast glorified my self!' (GA 96, 1 April 1907) which corresponds exactly to the translation of the Aramaic words that were actually cried out. It became clear through the explanation of how the two Hebrew words *sabachtani* and *shevachtani* are spelled, that the cry possessed a certain ambiguity, both words in Hebrew being written the same. It was shown that both translations, 'My God, my God, why hast thou forsaken me?' as well as 'My God, my God, how thou hast raised me!' are fully legitimate. However, the new possibility of developing the human self in freedom is expressed through the cry, *'Eloi, Eloi, l'ma shevachtani!'*—'My God, my God, how thou hast raised me!'—at the climax of the divine sacrifice, at the moment of death. The majesty of the Resurrection is already being proclaimed in this cry, but it was uttered at the last moment of God's most intense agony as He penetrated human physical death.

We came to a halt at this point, but it is not right to leave this painful event from the Friday without our souls taking in what happened on the Saturday and Sunday that followed. The Mystery of the Friday can only be seen in connection with the descent into the abyss of the Earth and the Resurrection.

Today, as a result, I would like to try to give a few fragmentary indications of the events which led up to the Resurrection. You can approach this life-giving event, irradiating everything with its power, only if you have turned your spiritual gaze as well upon the descent into the depths of the Earth. You can hardly gain a truly living understanding of the last chapter of *The Philosophy of Freedom* without having first read the chapters which lead up to it. Similarly, you can hardly acquire a deeper understanding for the Mystery of the Resurrection, for the ascent, if you wish beforehand to omit any work on understanding the descent just because this work has a somewhat bitter taste to it. This is the luciferic temptation in humans, to want to ascend to the higher realms of beauty straight away. What is valid for every human truly wishing to develop himself applies as well or even particularly to the mission of Christ: only the way of suffering, the stony path, the way through joy *and* suffering in all the bodies of man, leads to the Sun.

In the previous lecture it was intended to touch upon the path of man up to the death of Jesus Christ; in this lecture we shall turn our attention to what comes after the Crucifixion, and what for mankind can develop from it and from the Mysteries of the two days that follow it. This will also touch on the new initiation mentioned in the title to the last lecture. We have in the pre-Christian course of earthly development the vision of the incarnation of Christ, and in the time after Christ of His appearance in the etheric.

Now on the three decisive days of the Mystery of Golgotha very different processes take place, their differences even finding expression in the distinct ways they are perceived. The primary way the events of the Friday can be lived through is based on sensory perception. Here a form of exact experience of the physical events is meant which absolutely predominates over the supersensory form of perception. This form of perception was described in the lecture on 10 October 2004. Several elements of the last lecture were derived from this form of perception. Pure supersensible perception dominates quite clearly the events of Saturday. This experience stands in polarity to the experience of Friday. The events of Sunday unite these two kinds of perception. Sensory and supersensory merge into one another in such a way that the human being is thoroughly strengthened and penetrated in all his bodies. This already shows that the Resurrection represents the climax of all evolution, and that the previous events were necessary to be able to lead up to it.

Now, how are these three events connected with one another? The three days can be placed in a triangle:

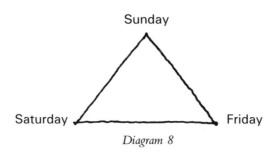

Diagram 8

What was already prefigured in the Awakening of Lazarus as a form of preparation for the actual event was actually constructed on these three days. The complete 'ideal human being' with all the elements of his being emerges, a being whom the human can contemplate as the crown of his own development, whom he himself should strive towards.

On these three days the basis was created for the development of the three higher members of man's being through the raising of the self. The following additions can be made to the triangle:

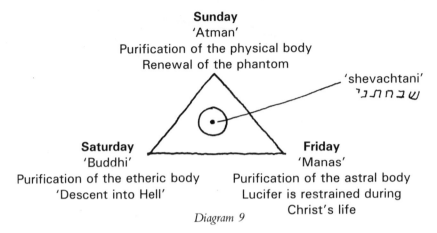

Sunday
'Atman'
Purification of the physical body
Renewal of the phantom

'shevachtani'
שׁבֿחתני

Saturday
'Buddhi'
Purification of the etheric body
'Descent into Hell'

Friday
'Manas'
Purification of the astral body
Lucifer is restrained during
Christ's life

Diagram 9

The purification of the astral body takes place on the Friday. It occurs while Jesus Christ is still living. On the Cross the blood of mankind, which had become egoistic through Lucifer, flows from out of the body of the Nathan Jesus. The purification of the astral body takes place on the Saturday. Christ descends into the abyss of the Earth putting Ahriman into chains as a result. The purification of the physical body shines out on the Sunday. The phantom is renewed. All this can only happen through the transformed, the 'raised' and 'glorified' self, which finds its spoken expression in human words in the cry '*Eloi, Eloi, l'ma shevachtani!*'

The prophetic symbol expressing the flow of movement arising from these processes is the Star of David. Coming from out of the divine world the human being is placed on the Earth with a physical body, etheric body and astral body. The self within him, which has become independent through the Mystery of Christ, can—by experiencing itself in death on the material Earth—find its way back again to its spiritual home. Through devotion to Christ it can perfect its various bodies (see diagram 10).

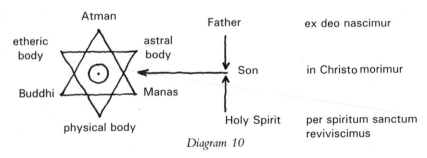

Atman   Father   ex deo nascimur

etheric   astral
body   body
                                Son   in Christo morimur

Buddhi   Manas

physical body   Holy Spirit   per spiritum sanctum
                                         reviviscimus

Diagram 10

The divine Trinity arises in the fully developed human being.

From this fundamental principle as well as from the days of the week and their meaning arises also the symbol of Christ containing all the planetary spirits (GA 104a, 22 April 1907).

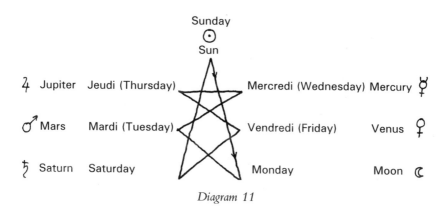

Diagram 11

Now we will consider what happens between the moment of death at 3 p.m. on Friday and the Resurrection on Sunday at 6 a.m. This first of all raises the question, why exactly did this amount of time elapse? Between these two polar events lie exactly thirty-nine hours. This is no coincidence. Considered esoterically the day ends at 6 p.m. As a result these thirty-nine hours can be further subdivided:

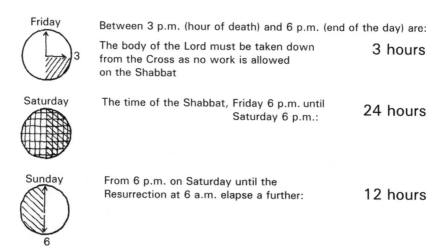

Diagram 12

For reasons of time we cannot go into more detail at this point concerning the significance of the different lengths of time of the three phases. However, within the context of the spiritual contemplation of Easter Saturday it ought to be pointed out that even in this outwardly measurable stretch of time (3 + 24 + 12 = 39) fundamental facts concerning the events taking place within the Mystery and about the future evolution of mankind lie hidden. Nothing within this Mystery happens randomly or accidentally. Everything that appears insignificant or unserious to someone in relation to the Mystery of Christ is in reality of absolutely major relevance. It is simply up to the human being's newly activated ability to understand if many things still remain a secret to him.

What now happens during these thirty-nine hours? In the credo it says: 'descended into the Kingdom of Death' or 'descended into Hell'. What does this 'Hell' mean? Is it just an idea of the world handed down from the Middle Ages? With the assistance of spiritual science the human being can indeed come to an understanding of these processes and experience that this term corresponds absolutely with reality. In order to arrive at a better understanding of the events, we can call upon two items of knowledge for support.

After dying on the Cross the divine, macrocosmic Christ Being permeates the nine layers of the Earth. Only after penetrating through to the core does the Christ Being in a certain sense fulfil His deed. The forces of Resurrection increase the deeper Christ penetrates matter. This is a truly painful process of struggle, requiring the power of a god, and is in the truest sense of the word 'hard work'. We children of men are only familiar with such hard work from our life and suffering between birth and death on the Earth.

Suffused with understanding for this difficult passage through the layers of the Earth, we can then deepen it by calling upon the second item of knowledge. For the Christ Being the 'basic development pattern' for life in this world and in the afterlife is, exactly, diametrically opposite to the human one. Rudolf Steiner refers in his lecture cycle *The Fifth Gospel* (GA 148) to this inversion.

The baptism of Christ is first the conception of Christ. The three years of Christ in the body of Jesus of Nazareth can be compared to the development of the embryo. The death of Jesus on the Cross is therefore the actual birth of Christ. Novalis understood this truth. He wrote in the fifth hymn from his *Hymns to the Night*: 'The birth hour of the new world drew near to him'.

Let us follow this development further: when the human being enters the spirit he loses his physical material body; for Christ the opposite is the case. When Christ ends His life's work He has merged so completely into the Earth that He can ultimately unite Himself with the Earth's surroundings. He first attains His physical body when He dies a human earthly death. Jesus 'the man' should not be confused here with Christ the god. In and after the death of Jesus the following applies: the human body belongs to Jesus, the body of the Earth itself, however, belongs to Christ.

The outcome of this is that the lifework of Christ unfolds from the time of the death of Jesus, in other words within these thirty-nine hours, and takes place completely within the Earth. In this 'Earth life' the Christ Being is hard at work making His arduous way through to reach His goal. He experiences directly all the entangled spiritual relationships of the Earth, goes through them, enters into their darkness. The Christ Being had already perceived all this from without, from the macro-cosmos, as a Sun Being. The necessity of holding Lucifer back and laying Ahriman in chains inside the Earth had aroused His compassion. That is why Christ had to take this path of sacrifice by becoming human. He had to die into the Earth in order to be able to encounter Ahriman. It has to be stressed that Christ did not have to take this path for His own development. It was because of His love for mankind that He accepted this path. In order to be able to help, though, He had to take this path into human death. The whole of His journey as Jesus of Nazareth, His betrayal, His torture, His suffering on the Cross—all of these had as their goal the events which happened within these three days.

In order now to indicate what kind of process of spiritual trans-formation took place in the depths of the Earth, I will have to speak in images. There are two reasons for this. First, the Mystery of Golgotha is and remains a 'Mystery'. As was already mentioned in the last lecture, the human being will only reach into this sphere with his under-standing at the end of his evolution on the Earth. To this extent any mention of these matters can be based only on a certain imperfect level of understanding. On the other hand, the responsibility is incumbent on precisely those individuals who live in the spirit of Anthroposophy and spiritual science to contribute in small steps, according to what is possible, to the revelation of this Mystery. In this respect many things still remain enigmatic and some can be represented in parables or images. The second reason why certain images have to be used when speaking about these matters is that the events on Easter Saturday can only be seen occultly. That is why anything said about them is always a kind of translation of spiritual facts. These facts originate in a spiritual cosmic sphere which exists without the need for earthly concepts. In this way any description of spiritual facts you wish to formulate intelligibly in your own words is always a compromise.

   The events belonging to the Mysteries of the Friday, the Saturday and the Sunday are also a smaller version of what the evolution of mankind on Earth represents on a larger scale:

Friday   Fall from Paradise into the material world, process of dying.
Saturday   Cycle of incarnations, development through suffering and
           experience.
Sunday   Ascent into the Heavenly Jerusalem through the ability to
           differentiate between good and evil.

This principle can, especially in relation to Easter Sunday, be elaborated even further, and become understandable with the help of a spiritual image. The Christ Being Himself passes through all the stages of evolution of the Earth in these thirty-nine hours.

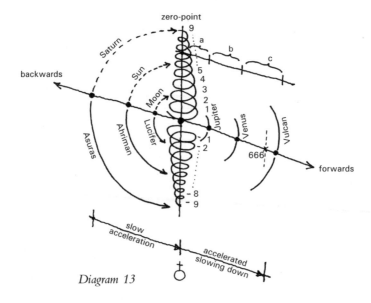

Diagram 13

The horizontal axis represents the planetary stages of the evolution of the Earth. At the same time the distances between the single incarnations of the Earth are different. The reason for this lies in the fact that the Mystery of Golgotha, which occurred during the incarnation of the Earth as the present-day planet Earth, represents the event with the most decisive influence, the turning-point within the evolution of mankind and the Earth. It is *the* most tremendous moment of fate influencing the evolution of mankind. All the subsequent planetary incarnations—which are awaiting us—only became possible through this moment. Around this moment, in other words close to this cosmic moment of intervention by the Sun, it is as if the course of evolution—measurable time is not necessarily meant by this—is now accelerating. The spiritual fact of the Mystery of Golgotha exerts a magnetic accelerating influence on the course of evolution. You could say, in relation to the Saturn, Sun and Moon stages which have already been passed through, that the course of evolution is slowly accelerating and in relation to the stages still to come, of Jupiter, Venus and Vulcan, that the rate of *slowing down* is accelerating. The influence of Lucifer within the evolution of mankind grew at such a rate that the sacrifice of Christ had to be accomplished before its time. The possibilities for development are potentially greater for that part of the future lying closer to this turning-point. As a consequence of the Son of Man's gift of freedom it is entirely up to mankind to develop itself consciously and with responsibility, to attain spiritual fulfilment and in the process restrain the dark powers—or not to do this. Since the beginning of the age of the consciousness soul you have to be realistic and recognize that serious decisions have already been made against the spirit which have produced and will produce circumstances in which the forces of evil can unfold their power. This calls to mind the words of Rudolf Steiner which say in summary: it did not have to come to this, but what happened was necessary (cf. GA 179, 2 December 1917). The further the course of evolution is from the time of Christ, the slower it unfolds, because the paths which have been travelled, the one ascending to the spirit, the other descending into spiritual decline—are distancing themselves more and more from one another.

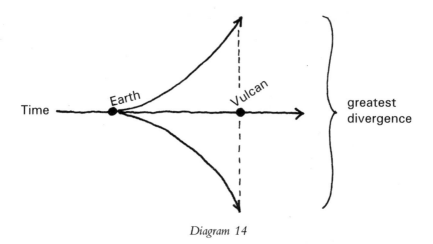

Diagram 14

This horizontal progression is connected with the spiral movement symbolizing the spiritual development to be passed through. Nine levels exist in the ascending and in the descending development respectively. Here a law of the spiritual world is revealed, a principle true for every form of development: where there is an ascent, there is also a descent. This is exactly what happened in the hours between the Death and Resurrection. Christ descended into the deepest material and spiritual abyss of the Earth, through everything in the abyss the Earth had acquired between the Saturn and the present-day Earth incarnation, in order from there to make His ascent. This is also the path of the neophyte. No spiritual ascent would ever occur without him previously having made acquaintance with the counterpart of what he is striving towards. Acquaintance means a true knowing and has absolutely nothing to do with sympathy for evil. Where there is a mountain, there is naturally also a valley, and whoever wishes to climb to the highest heights must be fully aware of the dangers of the deepest depths, otherwise a fall will cost him his life. The Christ Sun experienced precisely this descent, which is a prerequisite for the ascent. Here it no longer suffers human physical pain, it suffers the pain of the physical body of the Earth as well as the pain of the soul and spirit of the Earth.

Now the spirals are connected with the movement along the horizontal line because the nine layers of evolution of the abyss are permeated by beings who since the Saturn, Sun and Moon periods have remained behind, have not followed the positive course of divine evolution. These beings can be identified as luciferic, ahrimanic and asuric powers, and all are to be found in these layers of the Earth insofar as they have received a sub-astral, sub-etheric and sub-physical sphere of activity in the spiritual spiral. In diagram 13, if you draw a quarter circle from the Saturn point on the horizontal axis to the spiral, you will arrive in both directions at the highest as well as the lowest point, in both cases the ninth level. In relation to the past this is a certain zero-point, a starting point of development at which the dark asuric powers had already fallen out of the positive course of divine evolution. The ahrimanic powers are likewise placed at another level of the spiral or layer of the Earth because they fell away within the Sun incarnation of the Earth. And Lucifer and his hosts exist more at the start of this descending evolution as they did not fully complete their incarnation at the human level on the old Moon. For the present and the future the ninth level of the Abyss is also a zero point; in fact it is the terminal point of all (sub-spiritual) evolution. If someone consistently follows the path that turns away from the Christ impulse, he will one day meet the Sorat Being at this point (see diagram 13, p. 80),

Now in addition it must be said that these ascending and descending movements run parallel to one another, although only when the depths are reached is the ascent first possible. This appears at first somewhat confusing, but with a little flexibility of mind you can come to an understanding of it. The development process of the forces of Resurrection is always more complete the darker the depths the Christ Sun passes through. This actually means that there exist corresponding stages of ascent and descent. If Christ is in the sixth layer of the Earth and irradiates its darkness, He is as a consequence already on the sixth level of ascending development.

You can also experience and verify this phenomenon on a microcosmic level in this world. The esoteric exercises given by Rudolf Steiner, and which many of us practice, are aimed at the self gaining mastery over all unpurified astral, etheric and physical drives and cravings. The individual practising the exercises becomes aware of the animal that wells up in him daily. The exercises are then successful when thinking, feeling and will and the resulting behaviour are marked by the control of this inner animal. If he carries out the exercises conscientiously, the pupil will sense the moments when in his thinking, feeling or will, he is about to let his individual self come under the power of this animal. In this way he becomes acquainted with his own abyss, which at the same time can lead to control over this abyss. The ascending and descending movements take place parallel to one another, although knowing the inner abyss forms the prerequisite for any positive development. To be able to control the astral animal is the easier exercise for the pupil of the spirit; controlling the animal active in the physical is nowadays only possible in rare cases. That is also why the evolutionary ascent is all the higher the more intensive the self has to work at transformation.

Every principle of initiation conforms to this passage through the windings of the spiral. Whoever is able to consciously penetrate the spiritual world through intensive meditation or through 'waking in sleep' (cf. GA 10, Ch. 8) knows that what awaits him beyond the Guardian of the Threshold is no subjectively coloured, pleasant experience but an objective one. He also meets the 'accumulated debts' of mankind. He learns to recognize that the spiritual world—one is reminded of the Akashic Chronicle—contains not just his own abyss, which he definitely meets first, as the door to the spiritual world is to be seen in his own being. He also learns to recognize that everything essential is contained in the spiritual world, even that which is called bad when seen from a moral point of view. This has been 'deposited', in the truest sense of the word, in the spiritual layers of the Earth. When the neophyte has been permeated by this bitter realization (it is bitter, since to see what is lying and active in these layers is a true test of the neophyte) something even more terrible is revealed to him: in these abysses are not only the accumulated crimes and failures of humanity but also the karmic necessities to be met for balancing these crimes. These necessities consist of events in the future, which up to a certain point have to be considered inevitable, and which as a consequence *must* happen in order to achieve karmic balance. This includes not simply the small, individual karmic necessities but above all the wider karmic interconnections of groups, nations and the world. These future karmic necessities will have devastating consequences for the fate of millions of people and the highest integrity of soul and spirit is needed to withstand this 'vision' without being extinguished by it. The

1. *Damnation and Salvation* (1529) by Lucas Cranach the Elder,
Schlossmuseum, Gotha

2. *St. Francis of Assisi Receiving the Stigmata* (1319–1328) by Giotto, Bardi Chapel, Church of Santa Croce, Florence

3. *The Resurrection of Christ* (*c.* 1514) by Matthias Grünewald, Isenheim Altar,
Museum Unterlinden, Colmar

4. *The Transfiguration* (1520) by Raphael, Vatican Museum, Rome

guardian entity warns strongly again and again of this danger. Only the awareness of being in the objective course of world karma, and of bearing the suffering of others in the spirit of Christ in love and devotion, can carry a light into these abysses and impart the necessary strength to the neophyte for the ascent.

These insights are essential for understanding the descent of Christ into the abyss of the Earth. The possibility that the renewed phantom of the Son of Man will rise from out of the grave is only given when the descent into the core has been mastered and the ascent has been achieved. It is necessary to relate the essence of this Resurrection body with the descent into Hell, for this is where it is created. It has already been mentioned in the previous lectures that the phantom of the physical body was destroyed as the human being, through the luciferic temptation, sank down to Earth.

The following quotations from Rudolf Steiner from his lecture cycle *From Jesus to Christ* (GA 131, 10 October 1911) are intended as a help to understanding this unique body: 'Every Christian is therefore obliged to say to himself, because I come from Adam I have a perishable body like Adam; and with the right relationship to Christ I will receive from Christ, the second Adam, an imperishable body.' 'That which you treasure the most, the form of the human body, will not perish in the future; Christ is risen as the first of those who have been raised from the dead! The physical form of the body is not lost, but given back to mankind through the Resurrection of Christ!'

Finally Rudolf Steiner describes the relationship this second Adam body has to the physical body:

The more, however, humans develop clairvoyance in our time, the more one thing will become clear to them. The physical substances and forces deposited with the physical body are not the whole physical body; they would not even represent the whole form of the physical body. But something else belongs to these substances and forces which we are obliged to call, if we are speaking appropriately, the human 'phantom'. This phantom is the creative form of the human being, a weave of spirit which shapes the physical substances and forces so that it comes into the form which confronts us on the physical plane as the human being (GA 131, 10 October 1911).

Now if we reflect deeply on the following quotation from Rudolf Steiner we can find a further way to relate to the passage of Christ through the windings of the spiral and its connection with the course of evolution represented by the horizontal axis in diagram 13: 'If you ponder more deeply, do you believe that all the work carried out by the highest divine spirits through the Saturn, Sun and Moon periods only created something which is given over to the elements of the Earth at death? No! [...]: We know that the foundation, the seed so to speak of this phantom of the physical body was sown by the Thrones during the Saturn period [...] And so in order to understand the physical body we are obliged to return to the phantom' (GA 131, 10 October 1911).

This phantom and with it the physical body were already created on Saturn and so the way of the Christ Being leads through the nine spiritual layers of the Earth deep down into the Earth's spiritual legacy from the Saturn period (see diagram 13, p. 80). The phantom is therefore renewed by the Christ Being only when the penetration into the depths of the abyss is completed. For this reason no human beings who had died before the moment of renewal had carried such a phantom; they also did not have the basis for developing such a phantom. Rudolf Steiner has pointed out that before the Mystery of Golgotha Ahriman's influence on the human beings in the kingdom of the dead was considerably stronger than in physical life on Earth. In other words, through the influence of Lucifer, the physical body existed with a damaged or rather with no phantom and as soon as the human being died the elements making up the physical body dissolved and in the kingdom of the dead the human being came into Ahriman's sphere of influence. A reference to this can be found in the lecture cycle *From Jesus to Christ*: 'On no occasion had death ever been conquered by a human phantom which had experienced human death' (GA 131, 11 October 1911).

This applied to the time *before* the renewal of the phantom by Christ. Christ's renewal of this Resurrection body was the last chance to save mankind. Since then the human being passes through the spheres of the planets in his life after death and can regenerate himself for a new incarnation. The human self develops in these spheres a new astral body which eventually unites again with an etheric body. In this sense Christ can be understood as the Lord of Karma—for if Christ had not descended into the kingdom of Ahriman and laid his powers in chains, human beings would have reincarnated as egoists. They would have been egoists even before birth without having the free choice to become an egoist or not.

On this Easter Sunday Christ gave the human souls in the kingdom of the dead the seeds of the Resurrection body. He redeemed them from the impossibility of preparing their own karma, from the impossibility of attaining 'the right relationship to Christ' in order to put on the second Adam. He led the dead out of Ahriman's Earth sphere to the macrocosmic planetary spirits.

The chaining of Ahriman, occurring as the dead were awakened to the spirit, should not be imagined as some wild struggle. Rather Christ brings something into these depths of the abyss that Lucifer is lacking: a light of love penetrating through the rigidity and darkness. Christ does not carry any 'weapons' in order to battle against Ahriman, it is the love of this radiant child of God that lays the powers of Ahriman in chains. Ahriman is powerless against powerlessness.

The original Christmas night of *The Foundation Stone Meditation* is relevant at this point:

> The darkness of night prevailed no more,
> The clear light of day
> Shone into human souls

These occult processes unfold in the spiritual sphere of the Earth; they are not perceptible to the physical eye. Rudolf Steiner points out that the secrets of the Mystery of Golgotha are only to be seen with eyes of the spirit not by means of the earthly senses. That is why the life and the acts of Christ within these outward thirty-nine hours are hidden from the physical senses. If you express these thirty-nine hours in Hebrew as a word (each letter represents a number, several numbers produce one word) they give the word נל (*lat* 30 + 9) which means 'to veil'.

As already mentioned above, this life of Christ unfolds *inside* the Earth in a veiled form, with 'reversed characteristics' to the life of human beings on the Earth visible to the senses. Only an indication can be given of what happened during this descent into Hell. And neither should anyone be so shocked that it puts them off undertaking their own spiritual scientific study of this Easter Sunday. I would only like to say this much, that what accompanies us within our Earth, which at that time was laid in chains, is in no way pleasant and is not to be underestimated in any way. Only through facing these powers in full awareness and knowledge are they able to be controlled in any way or at least prevented from annihilating the whole of mankind. We do not want to condemn these powers of darkness as of course they also have some benefit for the development of mankind. The human being is put to the test by them. He can sharpen his awareness, and ultimately emancipate himself from them. However, the individual who lives contrary to the spirit feeds the power of these beings. One day they will break free from their confines, as they are becoming ever fatter—fed by every lie, by every feeling of hatred, envy, not only by every evil deed but by every evil impulse of thought, feeling and will as well. We were able to experience an example of this last Christmas[1] with the tsunami. The tremors are the rattling of the chains. And if someone says that because he wants to support goodness he will only concern himself with goodness, this is not in the spirit of goodness; it is blindness and leads to harm. Whoever wants to support goodness must be able to protect it and he can only do that when he knows the enemy and knows how it acts. Every initiation, every highly developed state of awareness is based on climbing a spiritual 'plateau' which opens up clairvoyant vision in *every* direction. It is the greatest temptation that the human wants to attain goodness straightaway without the bitter toil of recognizing the hindrances as realities and clearing them out the way. Lucifer and Ahriman are working here together. Lucifer promises mankind enlightenment and transcendence beyond the painful earthly path of awareness. Ahriman has made humans believe that the devil does not exist, that he is a myth of religious fanatics.

The Guardian of the Threshold warns us of both these paths and it is up to the human being himself to recognize that the power of these beings does not diminish as a result of them being ignored—on the contrary. These forces were so powerful that they forced the Sun Logos into the abyss.

---

[1] Christmas 2004.

Christ will reveal to mankind the secret of his remaining macro-cosmic bodies on the Jupiter, Venus and Vulcan incarnations of the Earth, when mankind will put on the phantom of Christ. The coming of the Antichrist while the human is still in the fourth incarnation of the Earth is then inevitable if he wishes to have these fifth, sixth and seventh bodies. The way Lucifer woos the human soul is by blinding him with the light of his grandiose delusions so that for many humans a world of illusion appears before their eyes and it becomes clear to them: 'Christ only gives me what belongs to the fourth incarnation of the Earth. Lucifer is actually much higher than Christ, as I can reach the goal faster with what he gives me.' *That* is the temptation! It is a temptation to believe that fundamental steps in development must not be worked for by the human being, that he is given these as a gift from beings he does not know and through processes of which he cannot become aware. This is an eminent way of preventing the development of the self. That is why, one day when you are so tired of all the problems, tired of practising the exercises, and expecting quicker results from yourself in the field of spiritual science, it is of great help to consider the immense path of sacrifice of the Christ Being and to let the realization flow through you that results only arise through steadfast faithfulness to the spirit. These results will be impressed—and here the human being has to bring himself to look beyond his current incarnation, into his next incarnation at the latest—like a seal into the substance of one's being. This can also be read in *Occult Science*. Faithfulness to the spirit can and must mean sacrifice. Comfort has to be sacrificed to the spirit, but the human being must also be prepared for a much more serious sacrifice. A sacrifice is always something one is prepared to make for an altruistic purpose. This is why a true increase in awareness will never result in a purely personal sense of satisfaction in someone. Only the hard path, with the readiness to help others as well as oneself and the deeply felt aspiration of wanting to advance the evolution of the Earth, will extinguish the sickness at the root of the desire to increase personal awareness in order to attain the goal ahead of someone less spiritually developed. A wholly selfless kind of joy arises through this readiness to make a sacrifice of love.

Christ gives Himself totally to this path of sacrifice for the Earth and for mankind. When He reaches the lowest point at the physical and spiritual core of the Earth He reaches the culmination of His sacrifice of love. The consequence of this journey through Hell is the Resurrection. The human being lives from it, we all live from it. The Resurrection conquers death—all the forces of becoming are created from it.

At dawn on the first day a light shone, rose up out of the grave and permeated all earthly matter. It is Christ Himself who merged with the Earth and became the source of love, became the eternal majestic fire. He is with mankind and will remain with it in a constantly metamorphosed form till the end of its days.

It is not the body of Jesus that ascends but the pure phantom, the pure Resurrection body. To be able to perceive the pure phantom without a physical body requires clairvoyant powers, which Mary Magdalene and the disciples had at their disposal. These powers were bestowed on them through the authentic and spiritual experience of the mighty images of the Crucifixion.

Rudolf Steiner says about the essence of the phantom in the lecture cycle *From Jesus to Christ* (GA 131, 11 October 1911): 'What the Rulers of Saturn, the Sun and the Moon had actually intended for the human being raised itself from the grave: the pure phantom of the physical body, with all the attributes of the physical body'. *With all the attributes* of the physical body is stated explicitly. This however does not mean that this Resurrection body is subject to the laws of the physical world, rather, as the spiritual and real archetype of the physical body, it is subject solely to the laws of the spiritual world. It does possess the stigmata, the sign of the path of sacrifice of Jesus Christ in which Thomas the doubter places his fingers. But it is so untouched by any form of physical bodily decay, that it requires clairvoyant vision to recognize Christ in this spirit body. Mary Magdalene first takes the Redeemer to be the gardener, and this is the way we are also to imagine the experience at Emmaus. At this point the fifth of the so-called basic exercises given by Rudolf Steiner is needed, the exercise in open-mindedness, which calls on the individual to save a tiny corner of his heart for the improbable but nonetheless possible in life.

Rudolf Steiner says at the close of his lecture cycle *The Gospel of John* concerning the ideas presented in the lectures: '... that which is first comprehended by the intellect is to condense into feelings and emotions' (GA 103, 31 May 1908). It is necessary in relation to the Mystery of Golgotha that the human being creates within himself a true and deep longing to understand this mystery. Anthroposophical spiritual science is our spiritual tool for this purpose. And so Thomas' lack of belief is not to be understood as a lack of religious belief. What is meant by this belief demanded by Christ is an awareness of spiritual facts.

With this in mind a quotation from the lecture cycle *The Gospel of John* shall round off these reflections:

> He [Christ] is there and He will return not in a form of the flesh but in such a form that the individuals who by then have developed themselves through the force of John's Gospel will be able to see Him, to really perceive Him and are no longer unbelieving if they possess the spiritual force to see Him. The mission of the Anthroposophical movement is to prepare that part of mankind which wants to let itself be prepared, for the return of Christ on Earth. This is the significance for world history of anthroposophical spiritual science: to prepare mankind and to keep its eyes open for when Christ appears active among mankind again in the sixth cultural period. [...] The Christian testament seems to find its implementation in the anthroposophical world view. In order to be led to true Christianity, mankind in the future will have to assimilate the spiritual teaching which the anthroposophical world view is able to provide. Many people are saying nowadays: Oh, Anthroposophy is something that actually contradicts true Christianity! But they are the little popes who want to make decisions about things they know nothing about, who want to make into a dogma that what they know nothing about does not exist.
>
> This intolerance will become even greater in the future and the greatest danger for Christianity will come from precisely that group of people who presently believe they can call themselves good Christians. The Christianity in spiritual science will be heavily attacked by these Christians-in-name. For all concepts will have to be changed if a true spiritual understanding of Christianity is to arise (GA 103, 31 May 1908).

So summing up it can be said: spiritual science 'does not want to lead to belief, but to knowledge (GA 103, 31 May 1908).

The Transfiguration on Mount Tabor and the last night on the Mount of Olives

6 March 2005

In order to refresh your memory and bring the events before your mind's eye, a few passages from the Gospels will be read out. These will also serve as the basis for the spiritual scientific explanation which follows:

The Transfiguration (Matthew 27:1–13)

And after six days Jesus taketh with him Peter and James, and John his brother and bringeth them up into a high mountain apart. And he was transfigured before them: and his face did shine as the sun, and his garments became white as the light. And behold, there appeared unto them Moses and Elijah talking with him. And Peter answered, and said unto Jesus, Lord it is good for us to be here: if thou wilt, I will make here three tabernacles; one for thee, and one for Moses, and one for Elijah. While he was yet speaking, behold, a bright cloud overshadowed them: and behold, a voice out of the cloud, saying, This is my beloved Son, in whom I am well pleased; hear ye him. And when the disciples heard it, they fell on their face, and were sore afraid. And Jesus came and touched them and said, Arise, and be not afraid. And lifting up their eyes, they saw no one, save Jesus only. And as they were coming down from the mountain, Jesus commanded them, saying, Tell the vision to no man, until the Son of Man be risen from the dead. And his disciples asked him, saying, Why then say the scribes that Elijah must first come? And he answered and said, Elijah indeed cometh, and shall restore all things: But I say unto you, that Elijah is come already, and they knew him not, but did unto him whatsoever they listed. Even so shall the Son of man also suffer of them. Then understood the disciples that he spake unto them of John the Baptist.

The night on the Mount of Olives (Mark 14:32–42)

> And they came unto a place which was named Gethsemane: and he saith unto his disciples, Sit ye here, while I pray. And he taketh with him Peter and James and John, and began to be greatly amazed, and sore troubled. And he saith unto them, My soul is exceeding sorrowful even unto death: abide ye here, and watch. And he went forward a little, and fell on the ground, and prayed that, if it were possible, the hour might pass away from him. And he said, Abba, Father, all things are possible unto thee; remove this cup from me: howbeit not what I will, but what thou wilt. And he cometh, and findeth them sleeping, and saith unto Peter, Simon, sleepest thou? couldest thou not watch one hour? Watch and pray, that ye enter not into temptation: the spirit indeed is willing, but the flesh is weak. And again he went away, and prayed, saying the same words. And again he came, and found them sleeping, for their eyes were very heavy; and they wist not what to answer him. And he cometh the third time, and saith unto them, Sleep on now, and take your rest: it is enough; the hour is come; behold the Son of man is betrayed into the hands of sinners. Arise, let us be going: behold, he that betrayeth me is at hand.

The night on the Mount of Olives (Luke 22:44)

> And being in agony he prayed more earnestly: and his sweat became as it were great drops of blood falling down upon the ground.

Dear Members and Friends!
Unfortunately at the previous lecture when I announced the theme for the next one, I did not consider the fact that it is not really possible to speak about the Resurrection in the appropriate manner when one is in the middle of the preparation for the Passion. When someone develops greater sensitivity for the mood of the Festivals his soul is attuned to the spiritual processes of the moment. It would be quite possible to say something about the Resurrection today, but you yourselves will be able to experience an even greater joy if we speak about it at the right time.

We have already spoken about the Descent into Hell in the last lecture, about that event in other words which directly precedes the Resurrection. However, as I do not wish to take up the thread directly from this event I will be taking a step back to the preparation for the Crucifixion and the Descent into Hell. This preparation in the night of Maundy Thursday to Good Friday is represented by the scene on the Mount of Olives described in the Gospels. In the reading of the text passages we have just heard the description of the night on the Mount of Olives from the Gospel of Mark. We do not experience much from the things unfolding during these hours. The reason for this lies in the fact that outwardly, for the senses, there is not a lot going on. However, tremendous processes in the spiritual world are going on for which the human being can develop his perception if he makes the mood just mentioned above come alive within him. And vice versa, if the human looks into the spiritual world at what happened in these hours, he prepares his soul with Christ for the events of Good Friday.

This preparation for the Mystery of Golgotha, however, can be traced back to another event which occurred much earlier and which can likewise hardly be understood outwardly: the Transfiguration on Mount Tabor. As this event expresses a kind of prefiguring of the Mystery of the new covenant which actually took place at the Resurrection, this may provide some small comfort for the alteration to the programme. This may sound humorous, but is basically to be taken seriously. Our consciousness soul is so far developed that with the comforting knowledge from the Transfiguration we can even summon up enough strength to accompany Christ on His path of sacrifice—in contrast to the disciples, who two thousand years ago had not yet developed in this sense any sureness of knowledge. The appearance and sacrifice of the Logos on the physical Earth is all about bringing the impulse to selfhood in human beings to the highest perfection. And because we today may call ourselves inner Christians—with this is not meant the belief in some form or other of institutional religious group—because we today can become His disciples by freely committing ourselves to Him, we are already participating with this decision in His revelation as well as in His path of sacrifice, which is the prerequisite for the revelation of His Mystery. We have opened our hearts to what this beloved Being underwent in a human body of flesh. We will be seeing how our possibilities differ from the possibilities of the disciples during the time of Christ's life.

Different individuals have completely different limits to what they can endure of the burdens of His path. Maybe one or the other of these limits will be reached. One person may have to leave the room when the death of Jesus Christ on the Cross is mentioned, although there would be no Resurrection for us without this cup from which He had to drink. One could even perhaps be secretly thinking that it would be much more preferable to hear something more edifying than accounts of Christ sweating tears of blood in the night on the Mount of Olives. But the fact must strike anyone who is aware of his own feelings that here mankind's task for the Earth period, namely the evolution of love, is being touched upon. If I am capable of giving perfect unselfish love to another individual human self, I will be sharing with total commitment in his suffering just as much as in his happiness. I would have no difficulty in devoting my sympathy to another person. The possibility of attaining this cosmos of love, the goal of Earth evolution, was born through the Son of God. We have not yet reached this goal. A sign of this is when our sympathy is pushed to its limits, when we are obliged to experience how many people at the present time actually isolate themselves from feeling compassion. Life has become a machinery for sinking into a lethargy of spirit and soul. How often do you not catch yourself eagerly attending lectures and meditating to acquire spiritual knowledge. But hardly a few hours later you are aware of being back in the daily rut again—or even worse, you are not aware of being there at all, since you do not even notice being back again. Generally, nowadays, the human being cannot endure very much. He is rapidly deadening himself. The only remedy for this deadening of the spirit and soul is not some form of purely intellectual, orthodox Anthroposophy but a spiritual science imbued completely with heart.

This evening two events from the life of Christ which are directly linked with one another will be considered from an anthroposophical viewpoint: the Transfiguration and the last night on the Mount of Olives.

In order first to attain a basic understanding you have to realize there would have been no reason for the Transfiguration if Christ's path of suffering were not an irrevocable fact within the Mystery of Golgotha. For the only reason why the Transfiguration took place is that the disciples should behold it, should experience it. Christ did not need to transfigure Himself for His own benefit. He did it for the disciples. And not just any disciples were involved; He had many more pupils other than the Twelve. He chose three disciples who should or could behold His glorification. He chose those who were best able to behold him in His transfigured state. These three had the best disposition of spirit and soul for receiving higher truths. Christ also instructed them not to tell anyone of their experience until after the Resurrection. The Resurrection is the moment in which the secret is revealed. Before this event it would be the unveiling of a Mystery that still lay in the future, that had not yet taken place. The Transfiguration is only a prefiguring of this Mystery. Only when it has been fulfilled and become a spiritual fact will it lead in every human being, in a wholly individual way, to transformation. Previously it was only the spiritual vision of three initiates of something that is to come for all men.

But why do the disciples experience His transfiguration? They experience His transfiguration because they will be made strong in their hearts, in their spirit, for the test that is in store for them when they one day will see Christ unconscious, mocked, tortured, crucified and deeply humiliated. They will be tested to see whether they can go this path with Him, whether their understanding is mature enough, whether they have developed their capacity to experience compassion, whether their will is strong enough. The Transfiguration shall give them the strength so that they do not fall into temptation when they are full of doubt and in fear of pain. That is the reason for the Transfiguration. This is also what the Gospels tell. They recount how Christ points out His imminent suffering to the disciples. He builds a bridge for them by saying first about Elijah, His herald, John the Baptist: 'They knew him not, but did unto him whatsoever they listed' (Matthew 17:12). The disciples know of course about the beheading of John and have realized through the Transfiguration, which they have just experienced, that with this the beheading of the reincarnation of the venerable prophet Elijah has taken place. 'Then understood the disciples that He spake unto them of John the Baptist'. And so they are able to gain some idea of what lies in store for Christ when He adds: 'Even so shall the Son of Man also suffer of them' (Matthew 17:13; Mark 9:12f). This is the account given by the Gospels according to Matthew and Mark.

If we look with the eyes of the spirit at these events on Mount Tabor it is clear that Christ vehemently speaks over and over again from His imminent suffering. He speaks about it in the spirit with the representatives of the Yahveh impulse as well as with His disciples. All His efforts are directed at impressing the image of His transfigured being into the disciples to arm them for what is to come. He reminds the three in the night before Good Friday, on the Mount of Olives, of this event of the Transfiguration. At this stage, in the night when He tests them, He demands steadfastness of spirit and soul.

We wish first to consider the Transfiguration. Again it must be pointed out that the only manner of investigation which comes into question is one which considers the actual events from the standpoint of spiritual science. It is only possible to gain an idea of these events if the content of the Gospels is understood not just as being about events that outwardly happen but above all about inner ones.

The Transfiguration must have occurred in early summer, the last summer Christ experienced in the body of Jesus. Shortly before, He had been in Bethany to celebrate the *Pesach* festival and had then travelled with His disciples to Galilee. The vegetation was lush, the fields were light green, it was quite warm, and according to the position of the Sun and the sunset it must have been in June. On this day Jesus took with him Jacob the Elder, Peter and John. Jacob—his name is *Jaakov*—who was not much older than the so-called Jacob the Younger, knew Jesus well from even before the baptism, in other words before Christ had merged with the body of Jesus. The mother of Jesus was friends with his mother or even related to her; she was called *Shloma*, in English Salome. She is one of the women who always accompanied the events surrounding Christ. He also took Peter with Him, who was actually called *Shimon*. He was a devoted person but quite rash. We will be seeing at the end what is meant by this rashness. And He takes with Him John, *Yochanan*, called *Yoche*. This is the John who at that time had not yet become Lazarus-John. He was the youngest. The great evangelist and writer of the Apocalypse still slumbered in him.

On this day for the first time these three were guided to a future form of vision. What they experienced in the initiation of the Transfiguration did occur in the night—the ancient initiation did originate after all from the Moon god Yahveh, but the etheric body did not have to leave the physical body as previously happened during the three-and-a-half day rituals of the ancient Mystery centres. It was a kind of interim initiation. Christ brought the three of them by means of His words and His presence into a particular spiritual state. They were only able to a limited extent to control this novel process of initiation themselves. They still had their teacher with them—Christ. Yet they experienced a completely innovative form of initiation. This degree of initiation is also designated by the phrase 'on the mountain'. They were indeed actually on a mountain, but Rudolf Steiner often explained that this phrase is also the designation for a transcendent spiritual state. In addition, Rudolf Steiner assigns 'historical significance' to these events on Mount Tabor (GA 139, 22 September 1912). The first manifestation of the new initiation occurred here.

Because the events now unfolded 'on the mountain', you can also only immerse yourself in these truly occult events in a higher state of consciousness. This is more possible for us than it was at the time for the disciples. They were living at the turning point in evolution and had direct contact with Christ Himself, but we should not forget that mankind was in darkness concerning its relationship to the reality of the spiritual world. What was still present were remnants of the cult of Yahveh and an awareness of the forefathers and the bloodline. But even the awareness of the forefathers, of the significance of the forefathers and of the spiritual place from which the forefathers originated, was only a memory and no longer living truth. Elijah had been born in John the Baptist to recall the origin of mankind and to prepare for the coming of Christ.

The state of rapture and bliss they were in became even more intense as they perceived the spiritual world in a totally new and overpowering way. Jesus Christ had prepared them for this moment in the many hours He had spoken to them about the archetypal impulse at the core of the human being, about what we today call the self. He led them back in a kind of vision to the beginnings of the world when the human being was still at home in the divine worlds and like a drop of water had liberated itself from the waters of the divine world, finally becoming denser but still carrying within the divine nature of its original home.

The secret of the Resurrection was then revealed to them, which was to take place through the Son of Man. It was an indescribable grace which the disciples were granted, and they experienced it as such as well. It was in the truest sense a state of rapture. Previously I always took exception to this word and held it to be an obsolete, exaggerated term. But it describes accurately a particular transcendent state of soul and spirit. This 'rapture' has nothing to do with the influence of Lucifer. The rapture of the disciples on Mount Tabor extended at that time to all of their bodies, physical and supersensible. The following example will clarify this: they climbed up the mountain around midday and came back down in the early hours of the next morning. In all this time they had eaten nothing. Christ had insisted on leaving the provisions in the valley, for he knew that the disciples would be nourished in the initiation experience from the higher hierarchies. And that is what happened. As the sun set, the spiritual Sun of the future was shining on them. Raphael expressed this in his work *The Transfiguration* in the rosy dawn depicted in the East, i.e. on the right-hand edge of the painting. The spiritual Sun stood in this way directly in front of the disciples, at first in flesh and blood, and then they saw Jesus completely in the spirit as the transformed Christ. Now I am obliged to use a phrase that sounds old-fashioned and somewhat too literal: the heavenly ladder, or the ladder of angels. It is in reality a very accurate image, because the initiate is turning to the hierarchies, his self ascends; and one after another the hierarchies turn to the initiate. They descend to a certain extent because the human being in his incarnated form still remains on the Earth. The disciples experienced for the first time the unceasing activity of the spiritual beings, how they serve one another and yet all still serve the One. This constant up and down, this active back and forth in all its glory and oneness, as though the basis for this activity were a group soul which could only arise from the highest level of selfhood of each spiritual being; this the disciples saw. Also to be seen in this sphere, with all of his purposeful will working towards the future, was the Archangel Michael. This impression had a particular impact on John. It was he who had a spiritual experience of the future Anthroposophia.

The disciples looked up into the devachanic world. They entered into a state of detachment from space and time. They were 'carried away'. At this stage they became aware of the beings of Moses and Elijah. You have to imagine the dialogue between the Christ Being and these two leaders of mankind in the proper way. It is not to be understood as a verbal conversation—in the way humans converse with one another in a definite language and with physical voices—it is a conversation between the individual selves, an exchange between beings residing in the spiritual world. The Moses Being recognized in Christ the impulse which in his time had worked through Yahveh and had freed the people from out of Egypt. They exchanged ideas about the significance of the Lamb for that time then and for the future, and about the immanent suffering of the true Lamb.

But why is it that the disciples saw precisely these two prophets? They saw them because they had prepared the way for Christ and consequently had contributed to actually making His glorification, His divine epiphany in a body belonging to the Jewish people possible.

Moses was the prophet of the Lamb. When he was active in the world in the personality of Moses, he brought his people an understanding of God the *I am*. He planted an impulse for the future, a seed in the group soul of his people, that they should not make *any* image of God, but seek and find His divinity in the *I am*, in their own inner being. Yet Moses was a herald in his world, an initiator. He was active in the age of the constellation of Taurus, and as he came down from the mountain with the tablets of stone his people had relapsed back into the Age of Taurus and had made themselves an image of the God who was to be found outside the inner being of man. The Golden Calf was its image. The period in which Moses was active demanded laws which the people had to follow. Moses had to wander with his people through the desert so that they could return to the imageless true God. Only through the necessity of obeying the Holy Commandments could the people gain any access to an understanding of Yahveh. They still had to be led.

The spiritual being of Moses appeared to the disciples as a preparer for Christ in so far as he spread the first truth concerning Yahveh, concerning the *I am*. As, later on, John went through the major initiation which enabled him to write the Apocalypse, the book of the future, he now perceived the whole significance of the Moses Being. In this occult vision it stood as a pillar supporting Christ in the watery element, the expression of the forces of the Moon out of which the human being had emerged. It was the representative of the heritage of the Old Moon, the cosmos of wisdom. (Please note the reflection of the barely visible Moon in Raphael's painting, which appears in the water in the left lower edge of the picture, lying in a direct vertical line beneath the Moses Being. See the colour plate.) Appearing to the disciples facing him is the being of Elijah, whose name already expresses his mission: the way to God. The El in Elohim appears in his name, which refers to his function as a representative of the Sun. This being was concerned in its incarnation as Elijah not only with renewing but also with developing the Yahveh principle. Elijah revitalized the old self through the new self, by helping the people to understand that the invisible, inner God was not responsible for the outer circumstances of life, that He was no longer a god of nature. Elijah, the preparer of Christ, was just as alone as the voice in the wilderness, John the Baptist. He also was an initiator at a time in which mankind desperately needed an impulse leading to an understanding of Christ. He brought the people a huge step closer to the birth of the individual self, along the path to the goal. John, the writer of the Apocalypse, perceived Elijah as a pillar supporting Christ standing on solid ground.

This image appeared to the initiate as the symbol of the pillars of Jachin and Boaz: Jachin/Moses—the pillar of wisdom; Boaz/Elijah—the pillar of strength. Together with the Sun of Christ who leads mankind to eternal life they form a unity. In this unity Rudolf Steiner discovered the saying of Christ: 'I am the way, the truth and the life' (GA 54, 1 February 1906). The Latin language retains the actual sequence: *lux, via, vita* / Moses, Elijah, Christ.

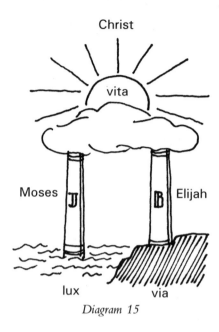

Diagram 15

The disciples participated passively in this spiritual dialogue by feeling the love and compassion of both prophets for the future fate of the Lamb. They were witnesses to this exchange.

Here as well the covenant was sealed between the Elijah Being, manifesting through John the Baptist, and the disciples. In this night, these three disciples, representing the other disciples, sealed a covenant with John the Baptist, whom they had recognized as the reincarnation of Elijah. From this day on, John the Baptist, the herald, prepared the souls of the disciples so that they were able to see in their own sub-conscious what they had been able to see through the spiritual eyes of the Baptist. In this way the interconnections of the events of the Mystery could become clear to them, following the awakening of their subconscious after the Resurrection. They were able to remember what the Baptist had perceived of the Mystery of Golgotha from the spiritual world. They remembered the spiritual events, the way he had seen them from the spiritual world. Even the images which they could associate with the events, for example of the Crucifixion, were likewise transmitted into their souls like memory images due to the presence of the spiritual bodies of the Baptist in Lazarus-John, who was the only disciple present at the Crucifixion.

They were able in this way to participate retrospectively in the events of the Friday and the other events.

From the moment of having the vision of the Elijah Being and becoming aware that he had reappeared in John the Baptist, they realized as well his significance and he became the spirit of their group soul, as Rudolf Steiner refers to him (cf. GA 139, 20. and 21 October 1912). He supported the Twelve after the initiation on the mountain, and was active in the development of their individual selfhood. From this moment on, and this can be read in the Gospels as well, Christ had higher expectations of the Twelve. He expected spiritual insight into His words, which He no longer couched in images, about the future covenant and the suffering soon to come. Only after the Resurrection and after the events at Whitsun did the help the disciples had received from the Baptist start to grow like a seed.

As finally Christ spoke in the spirit to and with the disciples about the glorification of the self on the Cross, He Himself was then glorified in His bodily nature, His self shone through the body of Jesus in a way similar to the Resurrection body. As His body was not yet like His earthly body after the Resurrection, He shone with a glittering blue-white light that was too bright for physical eyes. In Matthias Grünewald's depiction in the Isenheim Altar, the Resurrection body, the phantom body of Christ, is expressed through a warm blood-red and an equally warm golden sunlight. However at the same time Christ is rising up out of a blue-white robe with the same nuances of colour Raphael used in his picture of the Transfiguration. If you were to express the spiritual appearance of Christ in colours, then He was to be seen in exactly those colours which have just been described. And in this bright, totally sublime form, He was raised from the ground and the disciples with Him, and, turned towards the East, awaited the fate of the Cross that was to come with the rising of the Sun on the morning of Good Friday. He spread His arms out in such a way that one had the impression one was seeing the Crucified One, but not humiliated in the flesh—as this was a spiritual impression—but completely glorified, a victor of the spirit. The word 'transfiguration' means nothing other than 'glorification'. For the disciples the prevision that took place at the Transfiguration was exactly what the eye of the spirit can see at the Crucifixion: the glorification. For physical eyes the Crucifixion is a gruesome image, the manifestation of *sabach* (to forsake). For spiritual eyes it represents the victory that could be attained through the greatest divine sacrifice of love, the manifestation of *shevach* (to glorify). The victory is hidden in the sacrifice.

And His glory shone from the five future wounds gleaming and resplendent, as indicated by Grünewald in his picture of the Resurrection, as though all the glory of the Sun Logos at the moment of glorification through the Father God would no longer fit into the physical body. I have found a remark from Rudolf Steiner on this which exactly describes this event as an occult fact: the higher force of the self 'perforates', 'punctures', the physical body, which is no longer suitable for receiving the whole magnitude of the self (GA 139, 21 September 1921).

At this moment the disciples perceived the irrevocable confirmation of the Son by the powers of the Father. This 'voice' penetrated from an even higher sphere than the devachanic and they were unable to bear the perception. They sank into a lower state of awareness which is hinted at in the Gospels through the image of sleeping. Applying the concepts of Anthroposophy you can say they did not possess 'continuity of consciousness' (cf. the chapter of the same name in GA 10 *Knowledge of the Higher Worlds*). Afterwards, as well, they could not bring back over the threshold all they had seen into their waking consciousness. As a result they also forgot the knowledge of the Resurrection of the Lord 'questioning among themselves what the rising again from the dead should mean' (Mark 9:10).

Now what was different in the new Mysteries compared to the ancient Mysteries?

The Moon God, Yahveh, was to be superseded, human beings were to receive the direct influence of the spiritual Sun in order to develop love in their waking consciousness. Up to this point they could not see clairvoyantly at all with their individual selves, could not be fully aware of their individual self. Rudolf Steiner once pointed out how the influence of the Logos in pre-Christian times unfolded via the Moon. A simplified diagram illustrates this:

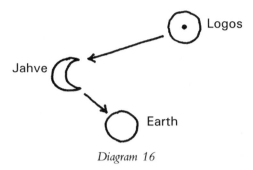

Diagram 16

The Mysteries of the Moon were now to be replaced by the Mysteries of the Sun. Christ Himself expressed it: 'I am the light of the world' (John 8:12). For the first time this Logos could flow directly to mankind. That is why the Mystery of Golgotha had to take place during the day, visible to the senses. The death on the Cross at the close of the day, the Resurrection at dawn. What was revealed to the senses had to be connected with what was hidden in the spirit.

Rudolf Steiner said in a public lecture on the new Mysteries: 'The belief in an afterlife was to be replaced by the direct knowledge that the eternal exists in the essence permeating the physical' (GA 54, 1 February 1906). This knowledge of the permeation of the physical by the eternal throws another light on earthly life. It demands that every single person takes responsibility for his own life and the concept of suffering acquires a new meaning as something that restores balance and heals. By developing our capacity for true compassion, the independent self, which can immerse itself in the self of another, awakes.

A few months later the time came for the glorification of the self. The possibility in the future of bringing the impulse to selfhood to perfection was prepared in the night on the Mount of Olives after the act of betrayal had been committed, after inaugurating the Mysteries of the Last Supper, but before the betrayal had run its final course.

As part of this preparation certain conditions had to be met and experienced by the Christ Being which were necessary for the way of sacrifice and its fulfilment:

1. Humans must have the cosmos of wisdom as their foundation.
2. The ties of blood have to dissolve in favour of the ties of karma.
3. Suffering must be recognized as a possible means of developing awareness; this means turning away from egoism.

4. The individual must confront the powers of evil. From now on there can no longer be any collective absolution of sins.

We shall be considering in a moment how these conditions were fulfilled in the night on the Mount of Olives. Before, however, I would like to refer to the congruence between the outer circumstances of the night on the Mount of Olives and the Transfiguration:

—Both events occurred in the evening or rather the night.

—Both times a 'mountain' was climbed. In His last night Christ actually climbed higher up the Mount of Olives as He usually did when He withdrew there with the disciples.

—Both times Christ entered a kind of cave beneath an overhang, an out-of-the-way place on the mountain. At the Transfiguration He took the three disciples with Him, because they were meant to see Him. In the night on the Mount of Olives He left them behind above the cave ledge as they were supposed to use what they had received from the Transfiguration independently.

—Both times a 'heavenly ladder' was to be seen; a direct and conscious connection with the Hierarchies took place.

—And on both times He took the disciples *Jaakov*, *Shimon* and *Yochanan*.

Here we have to take a brief pause. We know that the raising of Lazarus had taken place shortly before. Without today going into this initiation in more detail, we can stress that this 'new' John was initiated by Christ Himself—he had experienced a prefigurement of the new Mysteries. He was connected in a special way with Christ and since then his situation was different compared to the other disciples. He had received his higher spiritual bodies from the Elijah-Baptist being at his Awakening. Nevertheless we have to realize that the Gospel of John is the only one of the Gospels which does not give an account of either the Transfiguration nor explicitly of Jesus' preparation on the Mount of Olives. This will only be mentioned here briefly as this theme by itself would fill more than one evening. The writer of the Gospel of John and the Apocalypse, in other words the one who accompanied Christ on His last arduous path, did not really experience the Transfiguration. That is why *he* did not write about the Transfiguration. At that time he had been another person with a different level of awareness, an 'old' initiate. This memory of the Transfiguration was resting in his subconscious, deeply hidden, and in the night on the Mount of Olives he could just as little draw on the image of Christ's glorification for strength as Jacob and Simon Peter could— although through the Awakening he had developed an independently active self and a different capacity for love, which made it possible for him to be the only one of the disciples to stand until death at the side of his beloved Redeemer.

If you want to get some idea of the immensity of the Transfiguration then read Chapter 10 of the Apocalypse. There in words of the spirit is described what an initiate in the new Mysteries sees when the sustaining pillars of the new covenant appear to the eyes of the spirit. John beholds an entity whose 'legs', whose supporting spiritual pillars are Moses and Elijah, a being existing above the sphere of spirit (Devachan). In the Apocalypse we find the Transfiguration seen with the new awareness of the self. Active in John was the influence of the Baptist, the 'voice in the wilderness', who again was *before* his time. The fact that the Apocalypse is a book of the future is directly connected with the specific characteristics of Lazarus-John and of John the Baptist. These experiences made a deep impression on the spiritual bodies of these beings, a fact which is revealed later in Raphael's picture of the Transfiguration.

We shall now consider the preconditions just mentioned for Christ's path of sacrifice, two of which were worked through in the night on the Mount of Olives:

1. The foundation for spiritual understanding had to be the wisdom attained during the Moon incarnation. Through the initiation on Mount Tabor, through the spiritual encounter with Moses and Elijah, the three disciples received a deep impression of the reality of the ancient covenant and of the preparation for the new covenant by Yahveh, the *I am*.

2. The dissolution of the ties of blood in favour of karmic ties had been prepared. Here we shall only mention a few aspects which arise from a study of the lecture cycle *The Gospel of John* (GA 104) by Rudolf Steiner and from the spiritual experience of the historical events. In contrast to the Wedding at Cana, where water was changed into wine, Christ had served at the Last Supper, a few

hours previously, water—with an extremely small, almost symbolic drop of wine. He Himself drank nothing. The time had not yet come for pure water. Only beneath the Cross could He unite together His mother and John: 'Woman, behold, thy son!—Behold, thy mother' (John 19:25–27), shortly before the water flowed from His side. Jointly responsible for the 'sleep' on the Mount of Olives was the remnants of wine, of the old cult of Dionysus, as Rudolf Steiner calls it, which could only be completely discarded through the Mystery of Golgotha. Since the Resurrection humans should no longer consume alcohol any more as it leads them further and further away from entering the spiritual world consciously. The damage done to the supersensible bodies of the human being by alcohol in the time after Christ is extremely severe, as alcohol numbs the self and turns the etheric and the astral bodies into a horrible and grotesque caricature. So the self, whose physical carrier is the blood, cannot take the Christian path of initiation, and the ties of blood cannot be completely overcome. Christ had led his disciples to several situations where the ties of blood were overcome, for example through the meeting with the Samaritan women and during several teaching lessons, even in the Temple.

3. Still remaining was the sacrifice of Christ's suffering, not for Himself but for mankind. With His human will Jesus Christ had to prepare Himself for this in the night on the Mount of Olives. The disciples were only to a limited extent able to bear this suffering, as we will soon be seeing.

4. Linked to the prospect of this suffering is the confrontation with the powers of evil which constitutes the highest test in the initiation of a neophyte into the new Mysteries. The first human being on Earth to undergo this test was the Redeemer Himself—and in all His humanity.

In the night on the Mount of Olives Christ was obliged to undergo both of these last tests. Christ prepared Himself in this night to endure what had to come and He did this, and this must be stressed once again, in all His humanity. We know that shortly after the Baptism the Christ Spirit was still very independent of the physical and supersensible bodies of Jesus, but that over the course of the following three years this had increasingly changed. The Christ Spirit actually only penetrated the physical/material body totally at the moment of death. On the Mount of Olives He had already come very close to this perfect humanity, which is connected with all the powerlessness a human being can have. On the Mount of Olives the process of transformation does not yet involve the physical body but rather the etheric body and the astral body.

Let us stay a moment with the picture of all the temptations and all the sins which mankind has burdened itself with in the past, is burdening itself with in the present, will burden itself with in the future, descending on Him on this night on the Mount of Olives. Please try to imagine what this means. He was surrounded by all this sin, He took everything on to Himself. Everything dreadful penetrated Jesus the human being, right into the very depths of His humanity, neither corrupting Him nor making Him evil, but He appeared like a vessel completely filled with a terrible liquid. Try to imagine what a unique and immense impulse the Mystery of Golgotha gave to the whole evolution of the Earth and mankind. Try to bring the image of this immensity to life in you. With this spiritual and mental impression you will then be able to gain a vague idea of something else: that, namely, this divine impulse for the world could only be manifested through a sacrifice that had to be borne by a being of flesh and blood upon the physical Earth. The counterbalance to all the divine immensity of this Mystery is the same dimension of pain, the same terrible immensity of suffering.

The certainty that the sins of humanity would be manifested in physical torments threw Jesus into a dreadful state. You can also understand, then, why in this night the Gospels speak of Jesus warning of temptation, as it was the Tempter who was tempting Him as He appeared in the spiritual world. The Tempter sensed that because the humanity of Jesus predominated it was as if Christ had withdrawn. In this way it was easier for him to tempt Jesus as a human being. Putting it somewhat simply: he did not tempt God but Man.

On the inner retable of the Isenheim Altar the temptation of St Anthony is depicted. You can get an idea of the intensity of this event if you keep this picture in mind. It is also definitely no coincidence that Grünewald linked precisely this picture with the path of Christ.

But now what happens in the night on the Mount of Olives for the eye of the spirit? What is the spiritual meaning of the Gospel accounts?

We shall now attempt by means of brief references to at least throw some light on the actual events.

The time on the Mount of Olives can be divided into three parts. This is indicated in the Gospels by Jesus returning three times to the three disciples, something which did actually take place.

In these three phases three different spiritual states of Christ are manifested. (The following is the completed diagram which will be explained bit by bit.)

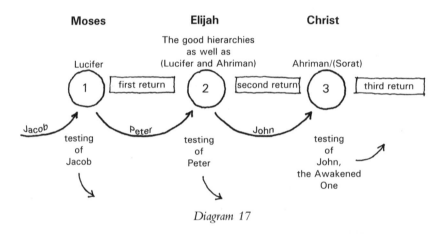

Diagram 17

Initially in the first phase Lucifer approached Christ and worked on influencing the astral body of Jesus. This temptation had to be undergone so that it could be overcome. Lucifer showed Him the magnitude of the sins of mankind in the past, the present and the future. The immensity is indescribable. Take for example your own accumulated 'sins' which are certainly not all that much, but even here you experience a feeling of unease and oppression. Even these personal 'sins' we all carry around with us and allow to increase in the course of our lives, even these Jesus Christ felt in these hours in His astral body. He was also encumbered with *our* load of sins. If we just ponder how much there is to overcome for just one life in the life after death, how difficult must it be to bear and overcome the sins of all of mankind?! A million times, a billion times more difficult. These sins are perceived in the spiritual world as living sub-spiritual beings who assailed Jesus Christ with a furious power. The only means to counter them, for Jesus Christ then as well as today for the neophyte of the spirit, is steadfastness in the spirit, unremitting focus on the goal, on the positive divine hierarchies. Your own Guardian of the Threshold is called upon to become active. That is why Jesus Christ is able to say: 'Not My will but Thy will be done'. This powerful affirmation made the luciferic powers uneasy. And yet these impressions do not leave Him untouched. So, bathed in sweat He stumbles in terrible anguish, due to the magnitude of sins, out of the cave to the disciples and wakes them up. He is afraid for the success of His mission because He sees that the disciples are not in a position to withstand the same temptation, namely the fear of what is to come.

He returns three times to the disciples. If you follow the events spiritually it emerges that He returns each time to a different disciple; each disciple representing a particular spiritual principle. Christ takes with Him consequently three disciples representing the bodies or rather the evolutionary stages of the human being. The first phase is the test that Jacob especially had to take (see diagram 17, stage 1). At the Transfiguration as well as in the night on the Mount of Olives, he represents namely the remaining disciples and their uncertainty. He represents the spirit of the pre-Christian group soul of all the disciples, he represents the men who did not climb the mountain. A special role fell to Peter and John within this group of disciples. So at this hour Jacob is tested within the group soul of Jesus' followers. After Christ comes to the three for the first time and actually speaks to Jacob according to his inner level of initiation, it becomes obvious that Jacob would not pass the test of remaining steadfast against the overwhelming vision of the sub-astral beings. Jacob sees Him in a spiritual, and ultimately in a physical state as well—a state that he and the eight other disciples cannot bear. It is the hardest time for the disciples. They feel abandoned by the Christ Being while He is preparing Himself for penetrating into the depths of matter. They feel they are now standing alone with new spiritual abilities which have to be developed. They have to find Christ within themselves, which before the Resurrection, however, they do not consciously succeed in doing. The disciples receive through Jacob the last instructions of their Master, which are basically that they should keep vigil in order not to fall into temp-

tation. In truth this vigil means developing continuity of consciousness, which we spoke about a little while ago. But even this instruction
is no familiar form of help as they have to maintain the vigil themselves. From this moment the eight disciples and Jacob abandon in any
direct form the Mystery process (see diagram 17, stage 1, p. 110).
Disturbed and lost, Jacob asks Him if he should fetch the other eight.
But Jesus Christ makes it very clear to him that they are too weak and
have not seen Him in His transfigured state. The appeal for awareness
of this prevision on Mount Tabor of His glorification is directed
especially at Peter (and John) which is why He also wakes Peter up (cf.
Mark 14:37).

The second phase during these hours is the centre between two
subspiritual poles. A heavenly ladder reappears. The hierarchies show
the Redeemer the pure human phantom before the Fall and afterwards the effects of luciferic evolution, the destruction of the pure
archetypal Adam. It was also shown Him that the only way this purity
could be renewed was by redeeming this dreadful reality, which had
previously been shown Him by Lucifer. This was in truth the second
major test for Him. He did rise in His awareness to the good hierarchies but in His humanity He came to understand through them that
this reality could only be redeemed, expiated, by a sacrifice on a similar
scale. His fear of the magnitude of the sacrifice grew out of this, for he
saw how much there was to be redeemed. This was not the direct
result of the workings of the Tempter, as it does not fall within his
sphere to show the way to redemption. This radiated towards Him
from out of His own Christ sphere of the Sun. So He no longer felt
only horror at the awfulness and vast amount of sins, but horror at
seeing how they had to be redeemed, horror at the vision of the
physical suffering. After that, the first sweat of blood appeared on His
forehead. As the powers of evil felt this horror, this fear, it was no
longer solely the luciferic Tempter who was active, but Ahriman as
well in his kingdom. He tempted Jesus in His etheric body, by seeking
to plant in Him a reluctance to take this path and bear this
immeasurable suffering. Ahriman's challenge was ingenious in its
perfidiousness. Ahriman asked Him what would be gained by this
sacrifice. He pointed to the future and revealed everything horrible the
future would in fact bring. But it was not the whole truth, for he only

showed Him the future from one angle, leaving out the positive side of evolution, so that basically it was untrue. Although everything he showed Him was true. Ahriman showed Him the future ingratitude of humanity, the abuse of His new Mysteries, the unchristian acts of human beings who would turn His teachings upside down in His name. He was obliged to see the false Messiahs. He had to see the hosts of angels drawing back in resignation. He perceived in all its tragedy how, despite His sacrifice, only a few individuals had developed the necessary organs of the spirit, how the Christ impulse was first submerged and was then reduced deliberately to absurdity. He saw the false teachings of the future, how they were turned against the spirit and saw whole peoples turn away from Him. He beheld the destruction of His sacrificed bodies, the destruction of nature, of the Earth, of Christ's body itself, and he had to see how all those nations degenerated who had remained founded on the principle of the blood—because they had not grasped the impulse of the individual self and had not become societies consisting of single individual selves— and how all these nations mutually annihilated one another. He beheld the small diminishing number of those who had taken a path of true Christian evolution at the end of the Earth period. All this Ahriman showed Him and linked this horrible vision with the accusation that all this evil would only accrue through the descent of Christ onto the Earth, implying as a result that He was guilty for all the evil. Ahriman knew nothing about human freedom, which would only become possible through Christ, but he sensed that with Christ's readiness to sacrifice Himself for mankind and freedom, his possibilities for using his power would also be different; that he would not be lacking—as the vision of the future showed—in human servants, but that he would never be able to extend his rule over *all* of mankind.

Blood was just flowing down the face of Jesus.

But at that moment as He inwardly reaffirmed the will of the Father during this experience; despite all the immeasurable suffering in store for Himself and for humanity, a cosmic moment arrived: His spirit united with the stars and at that instant Yahveh left the moon. This manifested itself in a dark spot in the centre of the almost full moon, and out of this dark spot came a Being of light. It was as if the God Yahveh were redeemed from His darkness, His being a source of indirect light, and at the moment when the Logos said yes to His sacrifice, He left the Moon shining anew for the spiritual Sun. His departure was like the pangs of birth and Jesus uttered a loud cry.

That was the moment at which Peter dropped out of the spiritual experience (see diagram 17, phase 2, p. 110). As Jesus returned to the disciples the second time with blood streaming over His feet and hands, He returned because He had perceived the spiritual unconsciousness of *Shimon* caused by the sudden exit of Yahveh from the Moon, by the final death knell of the ancient covenant. Simon Peter was deeply shaken psychologically by the imminent sufferings of Christ's sacrifice which he had seen in the spirit, and there arose in him an aversion to the truth that only from such a sacrifice could something new arise. In this way he resisted the path Jesus Christ was prepared to take. In contrast to Jacob, Simon Peter was tempted solely within himself. His spiritual and mental state is characterized above all by his repeated denial. It was not possible for him consciously to bear the way of the Cross and the death of Jesus. The second test was for the representation of the struggle of the human being within himself. Simon Peter had to lead a struggle within his self, while Jacob still stood completely within the Mysteries of Yahveh, and represented the struggle for the self in the group soul.

We can recognize how in this night on the mount of Olives the principles represented by the devachanic figures of Moses and Elijah, who appeared at the Transfiguration, experience a transformation. Both impulses appear in this night: the ancient Moon wisdom, Moses, the truth and the strength of the Sun, Elijah, the way. They encounter the three disciples again or rather the spiritual manifestation of each being encounters one special representative.

After this break, John brought the Redeemer back again to the cave. Jesus Christ was in a condition similar to death. The total reality of the spiritual bodies became manifest to the senses. The experiences in the astral body and the life body by themselves had led to such a physical condition.

With His last ounce of strength Jesus Christ finally plunged into the kingdom of the Abyss, anticipating what would ultimately take place in reality in the descent into Hell. The struggle in His human etheric body in the sphere where Ahriman rules led Him into the final depths of the Abyss. Everything that was explained in the last lecture about the Descent into Hell was seen in this test in a vision. But something occurred unexpectedly that is in fact a deep truth, a cosmic law, that Goethe also revealed in *Faust* when Mephistopheles says he is 'A part of that power/always wanting evil, and always creating good' (J.W. Goethe, *Faust* V. 1335 f.). For as Jesus Christ was obliged to look into the kingdom of Ahriman, and into what lies beyond this Abyss, there arose to meet Him the waiting loving souls of His parents, of the prophets, of the Baptist and of other familiar individuals who had died. Those souls also rose upwards who in the future through His appearance would die in total devotion to Him, such as His disciples, Mary Magdalene and many more souls of human beings in times to come.

This spiritual perception is not easy to put into words and again only images which come closest to the actual phenomenon can be used. These many individuals were the crowning point of the impulse to individual selfhood. Their individual, loving devotion, their sacrifice of love to the Trinity, ascended like spiritual flowers, each one unique in its beauty generating life and creating spirit as they unfolded their blossom. All these flowers arose from Christ's Sun of Love, from the sacrifice He would render in His human body. Only through His final acceptance of the cup could all the future loving spiritual flowers develop and grow at all. This vision of the loving and beloved souls in Ahriman's kingdom, who were all waiting patiently for Him, for redemption through His sacrifice, gave Him fresh inspiration. His powers of love acquired such a quality that ultimately made it possible for Him to take the path to Golgotha with a heart full of forgiveness for His tormentors. This demonstrates the impact of the cosmic law that something which appears terrible to the human being from the perspective of Maya, the illusionary world of the senses in which the human being is asleep with his will, is seen to come from divine goodness when he penetrates into the world of the spirit with awareness. For when the veil of illusion is lifted the seeker is left standing in the spirit before the naked facts of the spiritual world, which are mostly very uncomfortable—just as Jesus Christ stood at that time before the recognition of the necessity for the redemption of sins through Him. For every pupil of the spirit the following also applies: initiation is no 'bed of roses'. Knowledge of the spirit is like John's description of the book of the Lamb in the Apocalypse: 'And it was in my mouth sweet as honey: and when I had eaten it, my belly was made bitter' (Revelation 10:10). But on the other hand cosmic law teaches that something good often comes from a confrontation with evil.

As this third test was overcome Jesus Christ experienced a short vision of the imminent suffering, down to the very last physically perceptible detail, unfolding with such breakneck speed like the review of our life that passes before our eyes at the moment of death.

After that an entity approached Him and handed Him the cup of the Last Supper, which He now accepted freely (on the previous evening, at the Last Supper, he did not drink anything from the cup). This was the turning-point. Strengthened and totally changed, calm and decisive, He returned for the third time to His disciples and called on them to await with Him what was to come.

He sounds pensive when He says: 'Sleep on now and take your rest', and immediately afterwards: 'It is enough; the hour is come; [...] Arise, let us be going' (Mark 14:42). Again what is here meant is the lack of continuity of consciousness in the disciples; they are to continue seeing in the sleep state of consciousness. The Son of Man has first to be delivered up so that individual self awareness can begin to take effect.

This third time, with the summons 'let us be going', He is basically speaking only to John (see diagram 17, phase 3, p. 110). John is the only one who possesses the power of the spirit and the heart to accompany Him from here on, to stand by Him in His last hours. John is not tempted like Jacob in the group soul, he is not tempted like Simon Peter in his individual self; he is the Awakened One, initiated by Christ Himself.

And when you read Chapter 17 of the Gospel of John you will find under the heading 'The farewell prayer of Jesus' or 'The High Priestly Prayer' put into words of the spirit, into almost mantra-like words, the quintessence of these three phases on the Mount of Olives just described. Here speaks, just as in his Apocalypse, an initiate into the new Mysteries by expressing the spiritual words of Jesus Christ in this way: 'I pray not for the world, but for those whom thou hast given me; for they are thine: And all things that are mine are thine, and thine are mine: and I am glorified in them. And I am no more in the world, and these are in the world, and I come to thee, Holy Father, keep them in thy name which thou hast given me, that they may be one, even as we are' (John 17:9–11).

The central sentence has been singled out in order to give some visual impact to the spiritual content:

I AM	GLORIFIED	IN THEM
		∞
The word	'shevachtani'	immersion in
becomes	שׁבחתני	another individual self
flesh	The exaltation	love-compassion-strength*

Diagram 18

John understands how Christ is speaking about those who wish to put on the phantom and who will be wearing the white garments of the Apocalypse. They are the ones who do not search for God outside themselves but within, and assume as a result the highest personal responsibility for themselves and their actions. The new Mysteries do not consist of mankind being led to the right path by submission to the law. The members of the new covenant follow their God freely. Here in addition is a quotation from one of Schiller's letters to Goethe: 'If we stay with the particular characteristic of Christianity which differentiates it from other monotheistic religions, then it lies in nothing other than the suspension of the law or the Kantian imperative, in whose place Christianity wishes to put a free disposition. In its pure form therefore it is a manifestation of morality or the becoming human of the sacred, and in this sense the only aesthetic religion' (17 August 1795).

This is the vision of Christ's baptism with fire—in contrast to John's baptism with water. This is the beginning of Anthroposophy! The baptism by fire is the beginning of anthroposophical spiritual science! Rudolf Steiner says in his lecture cycle *The Gospel of John*: 'The baptism

---

* The original German word order is *Ich bin in ihnen verherrlicht*, literally 'I am in them glorified' so that the lemiscate appearing under 'in them' is in the middle of the sentence and not at the end.

with the Holy Spirit however is a prophetic baptism, which points into the future' (GA 103, 23 May 1908). Please ponder a moment the idea of how much significance we should accord the personality of Rudolf Steiner who created the anthroposophical impulse and as a result prepared the human consciousness soul to perceive that Being who is first able to actually baptize with fire, namely the etheric Christ.

However, so that the conditions will prevail on the physical Earth that are necessary for our Age of the Archangel Michael, Christ had to offer Himself as a sacrifice. The cup had to be drunk, against Simon Peter's reluctance. Finally we will take a look at the text passages in which Simon Peter cuts off the ear of the servant. The writers of the Synoptic Gospels depict this incident from memory so to speak. John alone, however, whose awareness is not present in the 'sleep' state, describes the event quite exactly and with one decisive remark. He adds something which we do not find in the others:

Judas then, having received the band of soldiers, and officers from the chief priests and the Pharisees, cometh thither with lanterns and torches and weapons. Jesus therefore, knowing all the things that were coming upon him, went forth, and saith unto them, Whom seek ye? They answered him, Jesus of Nazareth. Jesus saith unto them, I am he. And Judas also, which betrayed him, was standing with them. When therefore he said unto them, I am he, they went backward, and fell to the ground. Again therefore he asked them, Whom seek ye? And they said, Jesus of Nazareth. Jesus answered, I told you that I am he: if therefore you seek me, let these go their way: That the word might be fulfilled which he spake, Of those whom thou hast given me I lost not one. Simon Peter therefore having a sword drew it, and struck the high priest's servant, and cut off his right ear. Now the servant's name was Malchus. Jesus therefore said unto Peter, Put up the sword into the sheath: the cup which the Father hath given me, shall I not drink it? (John 18:3–11).

This actually happened the way it is written. Christ is asked if He is Jesus of Nazareth. They hear the answer but do not understand it. The problem is one of awareness and not of hearing. The answer is so incomprehensible to them that they fall down and have to ask a second time.

The representatives of the ancient Mystery school resist the appearance of Christ. They resist the appearance of the Logos on the physical Earth, in the body of 'Jesus of Nazareth'. They are afraid of the approaching turning-point. Which is why they have no 'ear' for the teachings of Jesus Christ. And so the old priest Hannas, to whom Jesus Christ was brought for questioning, also asks about the teachings He was spreading. Christ says to him He had spoken openly everywhere. Hannas should then ask those who had heard Him. They could give him the information. Hannas is one of the people who did not understand Christ, who did not hear Him, although he was present a few times when Christ taught in the Temple. The priests symbolize the lack of freedom in the pre-Christian period, which is why the passage in the Gospels speaks of servants and slaves. All of the people are slaves who do not belong to the priestly caste, because they are without freedom being obliged to follow the law.

Peter wants to strike off this ear which is deaf to the true Mysteries. Here his rashness, which we have already mentioned before, comes to expression. He wants to force the spiritual leaders and the people to hear the living Word, the Christ. And now please pay attention to the seemingly peculiar remark: 'Now the servant's name was Malchus'. What reason could there be to mention the name of one of the many slaves? It has already been pointed out in other lectures that the writers of the Gospels, especially John, were well versed in the language of the ancient Jewish Mysteries. John is recording here an important event at the dawn of the turning-point in evolution. The sword of Simon Peter is sharp because he uses the Word of Christ in his mouth like a sword in his hand, the sharp double-edged sword (cf. Revelation 1:16). In the historical act the sharp word was accompanied by a slap on the ear. In Hebrew the word for a 'slap on the ear' begins with the letter 's'. Peter then strikes off the 's' from Malchus so that a new understanding can arise. When the 's' from Malchus is struck off a new word arises; instead of the 's' the next (and the last!) letter of the Hebrew alphabet, the 't', grows in its place. The slave 'Malchus' becomes the free *Malchut*. *Malchut* is the 'Kingdom' of God that will come to the Earth when mankind understands the Christ impulse, as is written in the Lord's Prayer: 'Thy Kingdom come'.

But a new ear does not grow that quickly. The cup must first be drunk before the Kingdom can come. Only through the sacrifice of love of the God in Man can a new ear be opened which can receive the Word of the living God within; only through this sacrifice can a new eye develop which can see the light shining into the darkness. Self-knowledge must ripen in the slave so that he can free himself from being controlled and led by his subconscious. Only through self-knowledge will the slave become free, and he has to achieve it himself, by his own efforts. When this happens no priests or slaves of the spirit are necessary anymore.

All this can only come about through the sacrificial suffering that Peter, whose awareness was not yet fully developed, wanted to avoid.

Rudolf Steiner said: 'The human being himself must create an organ so that he can bear suffering'. And he also said: 'Suffering develops the human being to a higher stage' (GA 97, 19 January 1907).

Nowadays, the commitment to Anthroposophy is somewhat like Peter's commitment to Christ at that time. For one thing we can assume that the easy way does not lead to the goal. For another we ought not to deny the spiritual world even when the outer world opposes it with all its might. True love, as it should be developed, as the goal of the evolution of the Earth, constantly involves a two-way relationship: we receive the strength for our soul and spirit from Christ's glorification in order not to deny Him and His Kingdom, which at the same time strengthens the light itself shining into the darkness.

The Easter event at the time of Christ

10 April 2005

Dear Members, dear Friends,

When speaking to you today about the Resurrection, the highest and holiest and most healing event that has ever happened to humanity, this is more difficult to describe than anything I have already discussed concerning the Transfiguration, the night on the Mount of Olives, the Crucifixion and the descent into Hell.

There are several reasons for this. One reason is the one John gives at the end of his Gospel when he says: 'If they should be written every one, I suppose that even the world itself would not contain the books that should be written' (John 21:25).

This is the problem I am now facing as I have to make a choice about what I shall say to you this evening in this short time about this event in humanity's evolution.

It is namely—irrespective where you begin and which aspect you concentrate on—like wanting to remove a small thread from a wonderful woollen blanket and as soon as you start to pull on it, you realize that the whole blanket is unravelling.

This is a clumsy comparison but is to a certain extent a symbol for the Resurrection. Just imagine how not just the smallest action we perform in our life on Earth, but also every single one of our thoughts represents a spiritual reality and impinges not just on the development of our own personality but also on the development of all earthly reality. Rudolf Steiner often said: 'Even thoughts are not duty-free' (e.g. GA 131, 13 October 1911). If you realize that every ever so tiny action, every ever so tiny feeling, every ever so tiny thought has a real effect in the world and in the cosmos, you can then imagine roughly the dimension every single detail of the Resurrection has—and that in relation to the evolution of the Earth and mankind from ancient Saturn to Vulcan. As soon as I pick out one single detail of importance there are thousands of others just as important attached to it as they are all linked to one another. They cannot stand alone at all because they form a whole, and this whole is again linked to the total evolution of the Earth. I just wish therefore to point out in advance that the things I will be saying today do in fact correspond to the truth, but they cannot be the whole truth, as the whole truth can never be told.

The second reason why this lecture is difficult is that everything I will be relating this evening constitutes for our present-day intellectual or rather scientific mode of thinking, a sheer provocation. Everything that happened on this Easter morning at the time of Christ leads every outer science which does not take the spirit as its foundation to a dead end. Things happen at the Resurrection which for present-day sensibilities are truly very difficult to stomach. This is because, as you will see shortly, during this event the sensory and the supersensory worlds intertwine as at no other point in the evolution of the Earth. I have tried in the previous lectures to point this phenomenon out. It is a fact that the historical events which happened at the level of the physical senses oppose the materialistic world view so much that they themselves almost appear to be supersensible. I am not able to spare you much with the details in this lecture because not one of the things I want to tell you is theoretical. Every event existed as an absolutely living physical fact. Everything had genuinely unfolded on the physical plane in this way. It is no parable, no pretty legend. They are the pure facts even if they may appear absurd. This means there is nothing metaphorical about them. Everything that happened certainly has two or many more meanings, but it happened physically and historically. Precisely because everything goes so much against our normal earthly experience it is very difficult to come to terms with the statement that everything did *truly* happen.

Although, however, much of what I will be telling makes great demands of you, you should strengthen yourself with the certainty that through Anthroposophy we are not left completely to our own resources when it comes to the facts of Christ's life and time. Everything has an explanation. Just because we are not in a position to comprehend everything does not mean that the facts of the matter are inexplicable and are therefore a kind of psychological metaphor or religious hyperbole and exaggeration of the Evangelists. I would like to call to mind the quotation from Paul: 'And if Christ hath not been raised, then is our preaching vain, your faith also is vain' (1 Corinthians 15:14).

Whoever says, therefore, that what I will be relating this evening is not logically tenable and scientifically unprovable, is correct. To explore this event the human being is obliged to separate himself from his sense-based thinking. What is demanded here is a 'thinking with the heart' that Rudolf Steiner was always calling for. Thinking with the heart, by the way, provides essentially more exact and more truthful results than brain-based thinking. Thinking with the heart recognizes the truth hidden behind the outward appearance. What has to be said about the Resurrection automatically reveals the whole Maya of the external world. I have decided first of all to relate something about the historical course of events, about the people who were there, what they experienced and how everything happened. This certainly makes sense as a foundation for those points we will be wanting to examine from the standpoint of spiritual science.

I would like to begin with the night from Saturday to Easter Sunday. Around two or three o'clock early in the morning, according to my estimate, there was a powerful earth tremor. This must have been the moment when Joseph of Aramathea escaped from the tower at the lower, west part of the city walls. He had been arrested and imprisoned on Friday night. I am not sure whether the stone roof of the tower collapsed directly as a result of this earth tremor or whether it happened by some other (spiritual) means. In either case Joseph of Aramathea was able to free himself and walked along the wall southwards around the city and climbed down a fixed ladder, at the third southern tower on the inside of the city walls, back into the city and walked to the house where the Last Supper had been held. When he arrived he gave an excited account of his escape. He was enlightened by the experience. It appeared to him as though he had perceived a shining messenger-like entity, who was acting totally in the service of the Lord. The other disciples heard what he said but they could not take it in properly; the joy of seeing him again was too much (they had thought he had already been killed) and on the other hand the sadness and sense of being lost because of the death of Jesus was also too much. Joseph ate a little something in a very great hurry then quickly packed a small bundle, but took no clothing, and headed off shortly afterwards. I believe he wanted to return to Aramathea and go into hiding at the homes of relatives or friends. Now we will turn our attention to the rock tomb of the Saviour. You must not imagine the tomb like a Northern or Central European one, but as a cave in which you can walk around, consisting of an anteroom and burial niche cut into the natural rock. A few steps lead down into a hollow in front of the entrance to the tomb. In the interior the burial niche is closed by an approximately one metre high round rock which can be rolled, which further seals off a grilled gate. The rock in which the burial cave is situated is a natural rock formation and so large that there is room for several tombs in it which have their entrances on different sides. The entrance to the tomb of Jesus, which Joseph of Aramathea had originally foreseen as his own final place of rest, faces the city and the Mount of Olives, in other words towards the rising Sun.

Shortly before this Earth tremor took place a few of the guards who were sitting at the tomb of Jesus had returned to the city to fetch provisions. Three guards remained behind, and Cassius. Cassius is the Roman officer who pierced the right side of the dead Jesus Christ with the lance. He is otherwise known under the name of Longinus. As he saw the blood and water flowing out of the side of the Lord he was converted, just like the captain of Arab descent who had already resigned his commission at the moment of Jesus' death and handed it over to Cassius.

Cassius had sat down directly in front of the entrance on the steps down to the hollow in front of the tomb in order from there to keep the dimly visible corpse in sight, which he was able to do as it was full moon. As the tremor occurred there was just *one* powerful movement of the Earth. It was no long-lasting earthquake but more like a jolt. Cassius tried to see if something had happened to the corpse. He could not recognize anything, but believed he was seeing just the burial cloths like an empty shell. That the body, however, had disappeared while the cloths still lay there as though wrapped around it, seemed too improbable to him and so he put himself at ease with the assurance that he was still seeing the outline of the cloths. He sat back down on the steps.

Rudolf Steiner describes in his lectures titled *The Fifth Gospel* (GA 148, 10 February 1914) that the burial cloths were folded together either by an earthquake or by a gust of wind caused by it. He says himself that he obtained these findings from the Akashic Chronicle and that they are in fact spiritually precise but in an outer sense could be somewhat imprecise. This I can confirm exactly. It actually happened the way Rudolf Steiner describes but the external circumstances and the chronological sequence are somewhat more differentiated or somewhat more distinct. Indeed the Gospels are reporting 'only' an exact as possible summary of these momentous events. They convey the most important facts in a somewhat abbreviated manner.

It was therefore no long-lasting tremor around two or three o'clock in the night but a powerful jolt, and afterwards the cloths still lay there and in exactly the same way they were wrapped originally around the corpse. They lay there like a shell only without anything inside—just as Cassius had actually seen them. They only rolled themselves together later. I will be returning to this.

Here we already have the first unacceptable incident for the present-day mind. It is relatively easy to understand that an Earth tremor led to the rock cracking and the corpse disappearing into this crack. But more difficult to believe that at the same moment the rock behaved in such a manner that afterwards no cracks or breaks could be seen. And then the corpse disappears but the cloths wound around it remain in place. The corpse in other words passed through the material of the cloths and sank into the Earth, while the cloths stayed where they were.

I cannot comment on all these phenomena in this lecture but no matter how improbable it sounds, this is what actually happened. And if I were to leave this out and cover it up it would not alter the fact that nevertheless this is the way it was.

To provide some emotional reassurance I would like to refer to a spiritual law which Rudolf Steiner repeatedly mentions in his lectures. It is the secret of the transformation of spirit into matter and matter into spiritual substance. This is also the Mystery of the Last Supper. Because of spiritual science we do not simply have to believe but can also become conscious of the fact that man exists in the unity of his inner with his outer being—that a unity exists between the body and the spirit. The Last Supper loses its significance if it is understood as a symbol; just like the texts of the Gospels. Whoever doubts the foundations of the Last Supper, this secret in other words of the transformation of spirit into matter, can only interpret the Resurrection as a legend. In the Resurrection the divine will is active which not only transforms matter but in fact generates it, which basically is one and the same principle. But we can also meet this spiritual law in other contexts. The manner in which my body, for example, is maintained is based on this principle. The spirit generates substance. Spirit is transformed into matter. For this reason this body exhibits no symptoms of deficiency, it does not lose weight; in fact at the moment it is even gaining a little weight. But in any case it is maintained by substances which are not supplied from without but are produced by something within.

In the Easter night something occurs which is based on this same law. There the corpse penetrates the material of the cloth. For the moment I would now like to speak further about the subsequent historical events.

Between five and six o'clock in the morning Mary Magdalene and three other women set off from the house where the Last Supper was held towards the garden where the tomb was situated. With her were Marjam, the mother of Jacob and John, the wealthy Salome from Galilee, who also owned a property in Jerusalem, and another woman whose name escapes me. On Good Friday they had nothing for the embalmment and for a dignified burial of the Lord and had therefore, at the close of the *Shabat*, in other words on Saturday evening, bought many expensive herbs, spices, flowers and oils in the city which in the night they had subsequently taken great pains to prepare. I would just like to mention that the ancient Jewish tradition of embalming should not be confused with the Egyptian cult of the mummy. Jewish embalming signifies more a form of homage to the dead and was not at all designed to preserve the body from decay.

The women had put a few things into cloths and placed other things in small containers and two larger vase-like vessels. With these things they now set off in the darkness (the Moon had set, the Sun had not yet risen). They were worried they would be caught in daylight.

While they were on their way another earthquake occurred. It was the Resurrection of the Lord. This time it was a real earthquake with loud rumbling whereupon the guards collapsed unconscious. Cassius had been stunned for only a short time but did not become unconscious and afterwards went carefully up to the entrance of the rock tomb. From there he could discern that the heavy stone had been rolled to the right. This was actually impossible as the stone which closed off the iron grilled gate to the burial niche could only be moved upwards towards the left side of the rock face by the power of at least two strong men. It moved in its own channel sunk into the ground before finally dropping into a depression—similar to the depression into which the stone rolls in front of the grilled gates—coming to rest at the deepest point. Like a sign for the overcoming of every natural law the stone was now resting on the right-hand wall of the antechamber.

Cassius carefully opened the iron gates to the burial niche and felt around in the darkness for the cloths. He found what he had seen a few hours before. The cloths still lay there exactly the way they had been wrapped around the body. He could even feel a few larger parts from the flowers and the leaves Joseph and Nicodemus had used for embalming. But the corpse itself had disappeared. He went out into the garden, hid himself behind a bush and waited to see if anything would happen. What however now occurred he would not be aware of. He was spiritually too weak. But he remained sitting there where he had hidden himself because he felt for certain that *something* would happen.

What now occurred was the Resurrection of our Saviour and this takes place as a real rhythm of the Earth and as a spiritual power, creating substance every Sunday anew in every single human being. At this moment the Saviour of the world revealed the whole immeasurable grandeur of His Love to the world with which He had completely united Himself, as well as with the human beings living on it. At this moment, as the Christ Spirit arises from the grave in the first Resurrection body, He merges into the innermost heart of every human soul. It is now up to us in humility, in devotion and in joy, to celebrate daily this inner core of holiness by becoming aware that *we ourselves* bear Him—the highest and most precious—*in us*. Through our awakened self-awareness we can finally achieve the right feeling of how precious the treasure is that lives in us—how with this true and exalted awareness we can cultivate our souls and our spirits with care and dignity! This is the meaning of the phrase: 'Christ in us'.

I do not even want to try and put into stammering words the perfection and all-penetrating warmth of fulfilment of this deed of love. You can develop a feeling for this from Novalis, but ultimately every individual heart must nurture its own relationship to this Sun Mystery totally alone.

It is a powerful experience to perceive as an occult event this hallowed moment at the turning-point of evolution; the way the perfectly developed Resurrection body of the Lord, having risen through the layers of the Earth Christ had penetrated, ascends out of the grave and rises upwards, while in response an entity representing a whole choir of helping higher spiritual beings descends a heavenly ladder to welcome it. In the Gospel of Matthew is written: 'For an angel of the Lord descended from heaven' (Matthew 28:2). This is true and did happen. He performed the will of the Lord as though everything had been predetermined and as if he held the stone like a toy solely by performing the will of Christ.

The new spirit body of Christ ascended from the grave but it did not have to bend down to come out through the gate of the tomb where the stone was rolled away, but floated through the rock forming the roof, right through the hardest matter till it was over the cave and the surrounding vegetation. Christ had penetrated the hardest state of matter at the Crucifixion in the body of Jesus and had ultimately conquered the deepest depths of matter in the Descent into Hell. The second Adam was now complete, the phantom of the physical body, in which the Christ Spirit rises from the Earth. This Resurrection, this moment of penetration of the rock, was actually the birth of the phantom. And although, as we know from Rudolf Steiner, the phantom possesses all the properties of the physical body, it is not bound by the laws of the earthly world. Christ therefore ascended right through the rock ceiling. He remained this way for a moment, which in itself was timeless—it was an indescribable impression, as if His glory was shining in all directions, as if His splendour was lighting up the whole world equally in all directions. But despite shining in all directions, in His radiant being, in His will was an impulse drawing Him towards the West. It cannot be conveyed in words how the

Christ Being arose out of the rock. It was the work He had carried out and completed in the layers of the Earth which now raised Him like a Phoenix from out of Himself, raised Him out of His own body, the Earth. He achieved this Himself.

In several lectures Rudolf Steiner describes diagrams from Johannes Kepler (GA 148, 13 January 1914) which consist among other things of a circle, a sphere in the centre of which the Father God is to be seen, while Christ forms the circumference of the circle, or alternatively the surface of the sphere and the Holy Spirit represents the connection between the two of them—in other words, the distance or the radius between the Father and the Son. This is quite a mathematical image which however is found to be confirmed at the moment of the Resurrection. Here lies hidden the secret of the microcosmos and the macrocosmos which is not to be divorced from the Mystery of the Resurrection. Speaking in these terms, therefore, as the corpse of Jesus was assimilated into the Earth, was merged into the Earth, the Holy Spirit wandered, the divine spirit wandered through the depths of the Earth (radius) and penetrated finally to the core (Father). At the Resurrection the true Son of Man rose from the grave, the second Adam, who could only be created and developed through the incarnation, the death, the Descent into Hell and the ascent from out of the depths of the Earth. This is the Son who merges into the circumference of the Earth, unites Himself totally with the Earth to become its 'surface'.

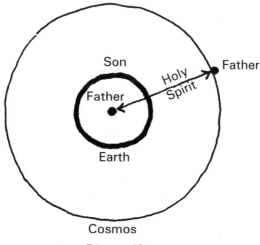

Cosmos

Diagram 19

Through the descent of the Sun Logos to Earth the macrocosmic force of the Sun united with the Earth itself. Which means that that which is called the Father God exists at the core of the Earth as well as in the cosmos beyond the Earth. You have to think of this spiritual cosmos, which here in diagram 19 I have to represent by the outer circle, more as being inverted outwardly. The forces of the Father basically exist behind this cosmos. God the Son is active in between, passing from one spiritual pole to the other along a kind of spiritual path, uniting the macrocosmos with the microcosmos. I had already mentioned this in the lecture on the Descent into Hell with the upward and downward winding spiral in diagram 13, the lower one symbolizing the descent through the Earth layers, the upper the ascent into the heights of the spirit. In that lecture we established that the development of the Resurrection body and the new role of the Logos in connection with the Earth occur through the simultaneous ascending and descending movement in the spiritual spheres. The result is that through the union of the spiritual Sun with the Earth every human being can become aware of his physical unity with the cosmos. Because, by having united itself with the Earth, the spiritual Sun lives in each human being who incarnates on this Earth. The will is the element in the human being that is the most 'asleep' and it can also be referred to as a force of the Father. As it is written in the Gospels: 'No-one cometh unto the Father except by me' (John 14:6). Gaining mastery of the will is the highest goal which can only be reached through Christ. For this reason we are able to understand that the human being is standing in the macrocosmos with his limbs, that every point in the cosmos is a centre for the movements of our limbs, as described by Rudolf Steiner in his *Study of Man* (GA 293, 1 September 1919). In our diagram we can also recognize how the human being represents through Christ (according to Kepler the 'surface') the central point between the microcosmos and the macrocosmos by being incarnated on the Earth and walking around on the surface of the Earth.

The moment at which Christ rises forth from the grave in His radiant Resurrection body is the all-important moment for the future evolution of mankind. But it is not just a decisive moment for humanity but is also an act of intervention of unique significance in the world of the Gods. That which the council of the Gods had once decided was implemented fully at this moment. The Gods planned a preliminary catharsis—the plan was to create for humans a balance to the influences coming from Lucifer and Ahriman—by Jesus Christ dying a human death. The Gods did not know this death on the Earth. This preliminary catharsis is expressed in the words of Jesus Christ on the Cross: 'It is finished' (John 19:30). But then the spiritual Sun had also penetrated into Ahriman's depths and by itself restored the spiritual body of the human being. This God appeared as a shining conqueror, a victor in the name of love. Whoever sees Him in this form can never doubt anymore, and this experience of His presence is not just for the one incarnation but also for all following incarnations—a sense of certainty, clearer, purer and stronger than all the physically provable things of the earthly world of the senses, which anyway disintegrate at death, like the material body itself, along with the earthly thoughts based on the physical brain. Spiritual thoughts, however, never disintegrate: 'spirit memory'—'spirit thought'—'spirit vision' (words from *The Foundation Stone Meditation*). They are drawn into the eternal nature of the human Higher Self and are active at the side of the hierarchies in the development of the new man.

The best way to create a mental image of this moment of the Resurrection is to meditate on the painting by Mathias Grünewald. A meditation on this picture has such a strong effect because it contains details that could only have been painted by an initiate. Even if someone does not intellectually understand everything, his higher soul, his divinity, of which he is unconscious, is aware of the moving truth in this work of art.

A whitish blue cloth is depicted, for example, and in such a way that it is easy to recognize that it lay previously in the grave. A large part of the cloth is still lying on the grave. This cloth, of course, also represents a spiritual phenomenon, as was mentioned at the part in the last lecture concerning the Transfiguration. But this picture shows in a wonderful way how outer and inner events work in parallel, about which I have often spoken. We have talked several times about sensory and supersensible facts directly combining and interweaving in the Resurrection. So this cloth is also outwardly the cloth which was at first wrapped around the corpse of Jesus in the grave.

Now I have to speak again about an event that has to be considered impossible by someone who thinks purely in a materialistic way: as the spirit body of Christ ascends from the grave the physical burial cloth is cast off for ever, physically and supersensibly. It is carried straight up as though by the wind; it floats upward with Christ as He moves up—I emphasize particularly that the material of the cloth penetrates the physical rock forming the burial cave—and falls back, rolled up into the burial niche after the ascent of Christ is completed. There it stays, the face cloth as well. The face cloth is the supersensible expression of the astral body of Jesus of Nazareth which withdrew through the head.

Again we can consider the painting by Matthias Grünewald. The neutralization of the laws of nature is brilliantly expressed by Grünewald in the image of a 'floating' tomb rock.

This is the moment of the Resurrection of Christ just as it happened on the combined physical and non-physical levels.

Meanwhile Mary Magdalene and the three women had passed through a gate in the south-west section of the city walls and had walked northwards following the city wall in the direction of Golgotha. The tomb garden lay south-west of Golgotha and a little beneath it in a depression in the landscape as seen from the city walls. There the women came to a stop, frightened because they saw the guards. Nevertheless Mary Magdalene went on up to the tomb, she was quite determined, although in the meantime she had realized that she had no one who would roll the stone to one side. Salome followed her to the tomb, while the other two women stayed up by the city walls and then wandered slowly and cautiously in the direction of Golgotha. Mary and Salome walked past the unconscious guards to the tomb. Salome stayed hesitantly on the steps in front of the entrance to the tomb. Mary however dared to enter the tomb. She saw the stone that had been rolled to the side, she perceived the spiritual entity which was still present and she caught sight of the cloths, which by now had been rolled up, without the corpse. As a result she dashed out of the cave, passed Salome without, I believe, saying one word, dropped the bundle she had brought along and ran as fast as she could out through the garden to the city wall and back into the city to the house where the Last Supper had been held. Salome had also realized that the body of Jesus no longer lay in the tomb and ran back to the other women to tell them the news.

Cassius, who had been awaiting expectantly for what would happen, had seen everything from his hiding-place and now ran in the direction of Golgotha to the city gate that was the quickest way to Pilate, to report to him what had taken place. In the process he crossed the path of the three women and hastily and excitedly told them what he had seen. As a result, the three women now also felt confident enough to go to the tomb. And there they perceived two spiritual beings. They were informed by these beings not to look for death, in other words not to seek the body but the spirit! They understood that they had to leave the tomb because it was the wrong place to be looking for the Lord. They therefore climbed back out again and went towards the city gate to wait for Mary Magdalene.

Meanwhile Mary Magdalene had arrived at the house of the Last Supper, woke Simon Peter and John up and told them everything. She was completely breathless, distraught and flustered. She had hardly finished reporting what she had seen when she ran back again out of the city as fast as she could in the direction of the tomb. Simon and John could not believe anything they had heard at all. But Mary's unusual and excited behaviour caused them to follow her.

Mary arrived at the tomb quite out of breath with tears running down her face and did not really dare to go in again. But she then perceived two spiritual beings in the burial niche, one at the head and one at the foot of where the corpse had lain. As far as I can remember she communicated verbally with these spiritual beings, at least she complained that the body of Jesus had disappeared. But she seemed hardly to be surprised at the appearance of these two spiritual beings, which can indeed be put down to the fact that she was totally immersed in the feeling of the close presence of Christ and was constantly looking around like someone harassed, as though He had to be standing there somewhere.

As she was running up and down in front of the tomb searching in despair and totally beside herself, she 'saw' with the daybreak against the rising Sun, which still stood behind the city walls—the garden lay a little lower than the city—a bright form appear behind a tree some six or seven yards away from the rock tomb. She was looking towards the east at this form. In retrospect it is obvious that at this moment sensory and non-sensory perception were mingling in her. In her excitement she thought it was the gardener, but seen against the rising Sun a purely physical form would never have appeared bright but dark. It was Christ in the Resurrection body. In response to his question whom she was seeking she answered that she was seeking her Master and wanted to fetch him back. Christ did not ask her for any arbitrary reason whom she was seeking, and also not to provoke her, which without thinking you could believe was the case, as He of course knew whom she was seeking, No, He asked her this question as a teacher of initiation asks his pupil. With this question He asked her if she was seeking *Jesus* or *Christ*. But initially she was only looking for Jesus of Nazareth, her beloved teacher in his physical body. But as Christ then touched her heart (in the Gospels this is when He called her by her name) she reacted immediately, so filled with love and so overwhelmed by the fact that she was standing in front of Him that she forgot everything. At this moment she even forgot that Jesus Christ her teacher had died, that he had died in front of her own eyes. At the moment of 'reunion' everything was forgotten; she believed He was by her again just as before. She fell down before Him full of love and wanted to kiss His feet.

This is the moment at which she is turned away. You should not think she cannot touch the body. She is to realize, just like the other women, that it is not the body of Jesus of Nazareth standing before her. 'Touch me not' (John 20:17)—she had forgotten the spiritual world in this moment, everything Christ had taught her about his return, and for a moment her spiritual perception was overshadowed by her effusive love. Nevertheless Mary had already developed her spiritual awareness so far that she could perceive Christ without seeing the stigmata. Spiritual laws are not tied to a sequence of circumstances as is imagined for the earthly world. In this case it is no 'deficit' on the part of Mary Magdalene that she does not see the stigmata. It does not mean that she *cannot* see the wounds. It means she does not need to see them to recognize Christ. It is enough that He directs a word of spirit towards her. (This was not enough for the disciples on the road to Emmaus.) She shall first touch Him, however, when He is united with the Father. This means *she* has to be aware of Him as united with the Father, in other words no longer as the incarnated human being *Yishoah*, but as the Risen Christ. For the human soul, Christ can only be recognized at all as the Resurrected One, as the Son of God, in union with the Father God (see also diagram 19, p.129).

It took a moment until the soul of Mary Magdalene had felt what her spirit had already seen—until she had a perfect impression of Christ in her soul and spirit. Of course, with the knowledge of the living Christ the longing to touch the body was also totally irrelevant and no longer present either. From this moment on she was left with the certainty of the presence of Christ in her heart.

What Christ meant is quite clearly expressed in the Gospel of John: 'Touch me not; for I am not yet ascended unto the Father: but go unto my brethren, and say to them, I ascend unto my Father and your Father, and my God and your God' (John 20:17).

John renders the words of Christ in such a way that the 'Christ in us' clearly emerges from them. Christ speaks about His *brethren*. Because they are His brethren, the Father God is not just His Father but through Him the Father God has actually become, in the light of the phantom body, the Father God of every human being. At the same time, therefore, He is His God as well as the God of every human being. The prayer Christ gave to the disciples when He was still in the body of Jesus, the Lord's Prayer, becomes here reality. Because Christ is 'in us' His Father is our Father. Taking a further look at the prayer where it says: 'Thy will be done, on Earth as it is in Heaven', and another glance at our diagram (see diagram 19, p.129), we have the forces of the Father appearing twice, namely in Heaven and on, or alternatively in, the Earth.

This encounter for Mary Magdalene is the beginning of a destiny of significance and promise for the future for mankind. We do not just hear any trivial request with the words 'but go unto my brethren, and say to them...', rather the clear instruction from the spiritual world, indeed from Christ Himself, goes out to them, the brothers of the Son of Man, and that means *all* of mankind, to become aware of His presence and His way in the spiritual world. Without in any way wanting to sound like a female emancipationist, I would like though to allow myself a little comment. It is a fact which does not fit into the ideas of the church, and the Pope, that Christ revealed Himself first to a woman of all people; He was able to reveal Himself to her because she bore the necessary maturity of psychic and spiritual awareness, and then to issue her with the task as well of speaking to the world about Him and His way. In the words which Christ directed at Mary Magdalene so shortly after His Resurrection, there already lies an indication of the imminent Ascension into Heaven, and even what is intended to be understood through the Whitsun event.

Mary Magdalene now ran in haste to the three women who had gone towards Golgotha. In the meantime John and Simon Peter had reached the tomb. John bent down in order to look into the tomb and saw the spiritual beings next to the burial niche. On seeing them he hesitated to enter the tomb. Simon, who did not perceive the beings, went by him and into the tomb. John finally followed him. Both caught a sight of the rolled-up cloths. In the Gospel of John is written: 'Then entered in therefore the other disciple also, which came first to the tomb, and he saw and believed. For as yet they knew not the scripture, that he must rise again from the dead' (John 20:8 f.).

This causal connection sounds contradictory. But it is not. With belief is meant that John believed Mary Magdalene, who had said the corpse was no longer there though the cloths were. That was what he initially believed. And then comes the sentence: 'For as yet they knew not the scripture, that he must rise again from the dead'. We have here two differing conditions: on the one hand the belief in the *I am,* and on the other hand the knowledge of the *I am*. The 'for' brings belief and knowledge in relationship to one another but in a relationship of opposites. This belief however was important for slowly comprehending what the Lord had said at the Transfiguration and at the Last Supper concerning the Resurrection. Seeing the cloths without the corpse was a preparation for John to then be able to perceive the Lord. Simon Peter now took the cloths and both retraced their steps, John running in front again.

The guards by this time had shaken themselves awake, stood up and were walking towards Golgotha through the city gate into the city, where they passed the three women who wanted to find Peter and John—for not only had they heard from Mary Magdalene that she had seen the Lord, but also that she had asked Peter and John beforehand to come to the tomb. This time Mary Magdalene walked back through the Golgotha gate into the city.

As now the three women also came into the tomb garden they also perceived the form of the Resurrected Christ. It was only a short encounter, but they also were filled for ever with inner strength, love and certainty. Overjoyed, like Mary Magdalene as well, they now walked back to the south-west gate and into the city and told the disciples that they had seen the Lord. Mary Magdalene had already arrived there. The disciples, however, did not really believe the women. But as Simon Peter and John returned they gradually began to believe as the two of them spoke in such moving terms of the events. Christ had also revealed Himself to Simon Peter and John as they were returning to the house of the Last Supper. But at first they had only perceived him in their souls, not with their spirit. As a result they had sensed Him but not seen Him.

That was now the approximate course of events on Easter night and Easter morning. I would now very much like to tell you about something that is not to be found in the Gospels and cannot be referred to as an outward historical event, but much more as a cosmic historical event. It is also important to speak about this in anthroposophical circles, you could even say, you can at first *only* speak about such things in anthroposophical circles.

Connected with the Mystery of Golgotha are three different perspectives on the events at the time of Christ:
1. the Gods' view of the events from the cosmos;
2. the view of incarnated humans, the contemporary witnesses on the Earth;
3. the view of the souls of those who had died before Christ, the humans in Ahriman's kingdom who were not incarnated at that point in time.

With a few general descriptions we now want to show how the cosmos and the dead in Ahriman's Kingdom participated in the Easter events.

I have just talked about a powerful Earth tremor taking place in the night, around two or three o'clock, and that as a result the corpse of Jesus was received into the Earth. However, a cosmic process is connected to this event.

The souls who were all imprisoned in Ahriman's Kingdom and had not experienced Christ's death and active influence on the Earth all had a vision at that moment of Christ's path of suffering and the places of His sacrifice, in other words, a vision basically of the whole Passion. I had already mentioned that these dead souls had encountered Jesus Christ in a kind of prevision in the night on the Mount of Olives. Through the after-experience of the Passion of Christ they understood what it meant that the Logos had entered into a human body and had died in this body. The corpse of Jesus could sink into the Earth and descend as far as the 'Earth's core' only through this after-experience by the souls of the dead of the process of the Passion, and similarly for the Christ Spirit, which was now separated from the corpse. It must be emphasized that the descent of the Christ Spirit through the layers of the Earth—this I have described in the lecture on the Descent into Hell—is different to the penetration and descent of the corpse into the Earth. They should not be confused with one another.

Through this after-experience the dead came to an understanding in their soul and spirit for the wounds and for the human death a God had gone through; all in all, therefore, an understanding for the assumption of suffering on behalf of others. With the help of certain hierarchies, they perceived the whole path of martyrdom of Jesus Christ in a spiritual experience, from the torture until the death on the Cross. They beheld all the stages in which pain had been inflicted on Christ through the betrayal. In their post-mortal state of awareness they were also led, so to speak, by the hierarchies to the places of suffering.

The events I have now described and will be describing were based on cosmic reality, which means they occurred in timelessness. What sounds like a long chain of events and seems to follow logically and orderly one after the other, subject to a chronological process, occurs in reality in a kind of mini-pralaya, and is simply enclosed by earthly time—in other words by a before and after. Within this timelessness an important event for the transformation of the Earth occurred as well.

A large number of entities went to all the places of the Passion and collected in an occult alchemical process the pieces of skin and flesh which had become detached, and the blood and sweat which had flowed from the body of Jesus through the tortures, the falls and His fears, and added these substances to the body of the Earth.

The simultaneous incorporation into the body of the Earth of those substances that had been separated and shed by these entities almost completed the alchemical process of transformation of the body of the Earth. It was real work for the hierarchies to fit everything together in the right way in order to make the new Earth 'complete'. If these substances from the body of Jesus (which descends into the Earth), that had been shed and separated before death, had not been added subsequently or simultaneously to the remaining embalmed body, the transformation would not have been completed. The 'lost' substances 'refilled' the damaged parts of the body.

What in fact was picked up by the hierarchies, in order to incorporate it into the etheric body of the Earth, were the etheric substances of the body of Jesus flowing out from the torture wounds. These are the seeds of etheric forces for the Earth and mankind, which are to help the Earth at some time to reach the Jupiter state.

Here we are obliged to touch upon a difficult area in spiritual science, the details of which still have to be gone into, but this can hardly be accomplished in one evening. But we should not leave it out completely.

The four basic elements which constitute the being of man, in other words, physical body, etheric body, astral body and the self, these four elements are each further subdivided. This means the etheric body, for example, is not a compact, homogenous form. You can express it this way, that the etheric body consists of different parts. You can say there are two essential parts to this etheric body, which behave differently in the sleeping state as well as following the moment of death and which have different destinies. It is impossible for us to go into this in detail this evening. But there are some brief references to this theme from Rudolf Steiner in his lecture cycle *Rosicrucian Wisdom* (GA 99). I would like to go into this now only in connection with the being of Jesus Christ. This must be done because the question can be asked quite justifiably why the Resurrection body of Christ bears the stigmata but not the extreme marks from the torture and the falls Jesus Christ was obliged to suffer. This has already been mentioned in the 'filling-up' of the torture wounds.

That part of the etheric forces of the body of Jesus which would go to the Sun as Buddhi, if the task it had to fulfil were a human one, enters into the Earth as far as the core, so that the Earth will receive the seed of the Sun forces. Alongside the etheric substances of the corpse these are the etheric substances from flesh, skin, blood and sweat. The other part of the etheric body permeates the aura of the Earth; it seems to disappear relatively quickly but in reality it spreads out and flows into the cosmic sphere of the Earth.

As a consequence there exists a difference between the wounds resulting from the torture and those from the Crucifixion.

We will first take a look at the blood, sweat and skin from the wounds resulting from the torture and the falls: this has to permeate into the Earth which will be the body of Christ. This part of the etheric body of the body of Jesus is active at the creation of the spiritual–physical body of Christ. The hierarchies gather up the etheric substances lost on the way of the Cross. These etheric substances have to be added to the corpse which is to be received into the Earth. What belonged to the physical body, and gave it a sheath-like form, must also become a sheath again, be gathered up and returned to the corpse and sink with it into the crack in the rock. These are the etheric forces which in an altered form prepare the new body, namely Christ's body of the Earth.

You always have to think of the Christ Being in an inverted way compared to the human being. In the lecture on the Descent into Hell I have already pointed out the phenomenon that the death of Jesus is not the death of Christ. The death of Jesus is the birth of Christ into the Earth. You could say that whereas the human is born into earthly life Christ is born into earthly death. This is the meaning of the phrase in *The Foundation Stone Meditation*: 'In Christ death becomes life'.

Therefore that part of the etheric body which sinks into the Earth is responsible for developing the new *physical* body, the body of Christ, and that is the Earth.

In this way the marks of the torture are not transferred to the phantom, which moulds the spiritual forces of the physical body, as the physical body has been made complete again by the hierarchies gathering the lost etheric substances together. (If you look again at the altar painting of Matthias Grünewald, there you will find the crucified Redeemer covered by the marks of torture, while the form of the Resurrected Christ—except for the five wounds—shines in a body which is intact.)

With the other, the second part of the etheric body, the situation is completely different. This is involved in the wonderful transformation of the Earth's aura. The blood from the nails of the crucifixion forms to a certain extent this second part of the etheric body. Rudolf Steiner mentions a few times how the spiritual face of the Earth was suddenly transformed as this blood flowed from the Cross and touched the Earth. Novalis writes in the fourth of his *Hymns to the Night*: 'Incombustible / stands the Cross, / Victory flag / Of our kind'. This blood transforms itself into pure etheric substance. This is what Rudolf Steiner is referring to with the term 'etherization of the blood' (cf. GA 130, 1 October 1911). It turns into etheric seed forces which permeate the ether of the Earth. The Crucifixion wounds remain on the Resurrection body, for they do not belong to what will constitute the Earth body of Christ. The wounds and the blood that flows out of them transform the etheric sphere of the Earth.

From the blood which flowed on the Cross nothing trickles down into the body of the Earth, nothing remains in the Earth. But, as this substance touches the Earth, it merges completely with the ether of the Earth and spreads out through it. As a result the ether of the Earth is given a new life, a total transformation. For the eye of the spirit it is comparable somewhat to seeing the etheric forces in a plant seed which carry the potential development into a mighty tree within them. In the same way, all the power of the transformation of the Earth into the spiritual Sun is present in these seed forces of the Christ.

A very profound and multilayered cosmic secret surrounds these stigmata. It will have to be enough for this evening to say that these stigmata are the channels for the etheric forces which radiate the Christ Spirit out into the sphere of the Earth. Even this we can find portrayed in a wonderfully moving way in the painting of the Resurrection from Matthias Grünewald.

The stigmata remain as the symbol of the Resurrection body, which is the spiritual archetype of the forces of the physical body. Because Christ had been at work on the spheres of Lucifer and Ahriman through the nailing to the Cross, the loss of blood and through death, these have become a part of the spiritual archetype of the physical body, the body of the future for mankind.

This is what took place within this mini-pralaya: the parts of the etheric body of the body of Jesus were picked up and these substances were then added to the corpse, which was then received into the Earth at the time of the Earth tremor.

Since the day of the Resurrection specific influences can emanate from the points of the stigmata in humans—for every human, even those who do not bear the stigmata in a way that is visible to the senses. To the extent that we 'bring ourselves into the right relationship to Christ' we put on and attract the 'new Adam' (1 Corinthians 15:45–49; Romans 5:14) which bears these stigmata (the German verb *anziehen* means 'to put on, to clothe' and 'to attract' like a magnet). We incorporate this Christ seed into us, bring it to flower through the devotion of our spirit and soul to Him. And the more this new garment, the new temple of man, resembles this Resurrection body the stronger the process becomes of unification of the human being with Christ. In his own individual way he is penetrated by the influence of this first phantom, which arose at that time from the grave. And for each one of us who 'brings himself into the right relationship with Christ' the corresponding points on the hands and the feet (the wound on the side as well) also acquire a highly important significance.

Because of the Resurrection, the human being can send his individual self, by means of the etheric body, out into the world from these points. At no other point on the body does the etheric body project so strongly into the outer world as the hands. If you look again more closely at the altar painting of Grünewald, you can then recognize the fine rays projecting from the stigmata. They shine like small suns. The sense of touch for human beings, for all of us, is weak at those points where the stigmata are located. But if we relax and tune in to our perceptions we have more a sense that these points radiate into the etheric the transformed substance of our own individual self; just like the sun sends out its rays. The human being can move around in his surroundings by means of the points of the stigmata on the palms and the backs of his hands, through totally new etheric sense organs. These are not weak, passively functioning sense organs, they exert a powerful influence if you cultivate and develop them. They are the condensed substance of your individual self actively radiating and giving. This is a significant transformation in the spirit of the Christ impulse, as it involves the active participation of the will in shaping the outer world.

The wounds on the feet are connected (in a completely different way from the hands) with the ground on which they 'tread'. They wish to meet it with a respect and love which grows from the awareness that the human being owes his consciousness and his freely made commitment to Christ to the fact that he has emerged as an incarnated being out of the fertile soil of the Earth, and also that only by experiencing his karma on this physical Earth can he develop a relationship to Christ within his own self.

Here again is to be said, and this is at once the simplest and the most important message of the secret of Easter: *Christ must be found in earthly life!—not after death. He can only be found after death, if He has been known in earthly life.* To explore the Resurrection in the spirit of Christ is to become familiar with Christ, whom we bear within us. This is the most direct way to an understanding of Christ after death.

I would have liked to have gone into the wound made by the spear which again holds a different secret. If you wish to continue researching along these lines Novalis can help you further (in the fifth of his *Hymns to the Night*): 'Eternal life was manifested in death—you are death and make us truly whole'. The most significant aspect of the spear wound, among others, is namely that blood and water flowed from it but after He had died!

The blood that flowed from the wounds of the stigmata on the hands and feet is therefore spiritually seen, different from the blood which flowed from the side wound. We know as anthroposophists that the blood is the physical vehicle of the individual self. It circulates through the living human being and in doing so bestows on him his living individual selfhood. If the human being is dead the blood no longer circulates. This means that the self withdraws from the human being. As a result it is a very significant and profound difference when on the Cross the blood flows from the hands and the feet of Christ incarnated in the body of Jesus and on the other hand when the blood flows from a wound to a body which is no longer permeated by the self, which is dead. What can also be of help here is if we imagine that the death of Jesus represents the birth of Christ.

The human being of the future will offer his entire pure and holy love to the Christ Being as a sacrificial offering. He will as a result be inwardly exalted. His soul will become beautiful, will receive the objective beauty of the cosmos. He will cultivate this love within himself as his highest aesthetic and ethical sensibility, as his most precious possession. He will never let this golden bud wither or go dry. He would not be able to do this anyway, as contact with the Saviour of the Sun and the Earth will be as natural to him as the present-day human breathes in the air. He will create an awareness for something which is anyway a fact without his being aware of it: Christ has united Himself with the Earth and as a result with mankind. Everything that goes to make up the external aspects of the human being in his physical existence can be traced back to the divine spirit which lives in the human being through the sacrifice of the Logos in descending onto and into the Earth. He will remodel his body from within out, turn it into a temple pure and beautiful enough to receive and consciously bear the holy of holies. But the light of the spirit must be experienced in a human body here on the Earth—in other words while incarnated. To become human means developing awareness. Only in this way is it possible to offer up the sacrifice.

Only he who has received into his heart the appearance of Christ at the turning-point of evolution and lives daily with this knowledge in his soul and spirit can develop a spirit organ for perceiving Him in the etheric world. Only he who stands in a valid relationship to the appearance of Christ at the turning-point of evolution, in other words, to the Logos in a human body, can develop a relationship to the etheric Christ. Otherwise it is of no help, however often someone goes to church or however many membership cards he carries around with him. He will never develop it. Whoever expects everything to be given him as a gift has not understood the Christ impulse. The gift is to give oneself actively and firmly, not half-heartedly and full of doubt but full of courage and devotion, without any expectation of gaining personal advantage from anyone as a result, but in order to help another person or all of mankind.

The Resurrection is an event that can actually only be understood by the spirit and the heart. All external science ends at this point. Someone nowadays who thinks in contemporary terms would not be able to understand the events, not just the supersensible events but also those perceptible to the senses, of the Resurrection. And that indeed is how it has to be. It should not be merely looked at in an external manner and only be provable in an external manner. The human being can only approach these secrets through the eye of the spirit.

Dominus mirabilia fecit is a saying from the Middle Ages. Nowadays we ought to be able to initially accept this 'wonder' as a fact in order, then, with the help of spiritual science, to slowly feel our way into it and arrive at a spiritual understanding of it.

The Mystery of Golgotha is not a subjective question of faith that either does or does not exist, it is an historical, objective living fact at the physical, soul and spirit levels!

If you delve into the wonderful events and secrets connected with the Crucifixion and the Descent into Hell the demands placed on your emotions are very high. The climax, the real test for your emotions and for your thinking, however, is everything connected with the Resurrection. With gratitude we are reminded of the exercise in open-mindedness given to us for our path by Rudolf Steiner. This time it is not a 'tiny corner' you will be needing to save in your heart, but a larger one. You have no doubt sensed how your brain was spinning and squirming from the descriptions given in the lectures. With normal patterns of thinking and explanation you will not get very far. The brain goes on strike. The human being is obliged, if he wants to progress, to activate a different form of thinking. And this is how it should be! Only in this way can it be guaranteed that the human being approaches the secrets of the Mystery of Golgotha in a dignified and meaningful way. We are dealing here not with the wondrous fate of some God deemed to be worthy of our adoration (it is that as well) but primarily with something that involves us and our development here on the Earth. This is of great significance for the human being. And that is why 'dead thinking', as Rudolf Steiner calls it, must be abandoned. You can follow how at precisely this point brain-based thinking is not agile enough in the face of these super-sensible truths. To draw near to the event of the Resurrection means, therefore, that the human being has to turn to what happened, has to surrender himself to Christ on a wholly personal and individual level, and totally alone. It is a genuine act of will for the human being to transform his dead thinking into living thinking. You yourselves will be able to feel, when you begin to involve yourself in the Resurrection, how after a while your brain is no longer able to handle the subject at all. However you will notice how a unique sensation arises. Compared to the normal processes of thinking your whole inner state is totally altered. It becomes truly alive, pulsating, and as soon as something like an intuition arises, there arises with it an inner sense which knows that the Gospels are speaking the truth. At such moments the human being burns with an irrefutable sense of certainty. At first he will be aware of a general change in his attitude, in his whole inner being towards the processes of this Mystery. But in whatever form this change occurs, gentle and delicate or like a fanfare of trumpets, this is the awakening of his Christ consciousness, the awareness of his true humanity. This is the beginning of his unique and living relationship with Christ.

The Whitsun event at the time of Christ and its connection with Anthroposophy

14 May 2005

Dear Members, dear Friends,

At the present time one has the impression that awareness of the Whitsun event, especially among the general public, is in decline and in terms of its significance lagging far behind the Feast of Easter. But even though the general understanding nowadays may be so limited and diluted, at least everyone still knows that Easter is Resurrection. But what lies hidden behind the Feast of Whitsun remains to a large extent completely abstract. Whitsun does at least still exist as a public holiday and is celebrated by most Christian religious communities, but even here nothing is really heard about the meaning of this feast. This is also no surprise as Whitsun is the birth of the conscious and free fourfold human being, is the birth of the free human being not only in the way it has given the fullness of grace of the Easter event to each human being, regardless of how he stands in relation to Christ, but is also the birth of the free human being in his astral body and in his individual self, in his soul and in his spirit. Because every human being must and above all can create by *himself* this connection to Christ in his soul and in his self, it is also clear that the outpouring of the Holy Spirit is not only intended for the disciples at the time of Christ, but can be for every person who is presently in the world. We will be going into this in closer detail afterwards. This conception of enlightenment is not held by the churches, because every person who is permeated by this spirit will also as a consequence be free from every institution— must basically be able to be a priest in the broadest sense of the word.

Whitsun experienced with awareness is spiritual science. If the churches were really to celebrate Whitsun, then they would be convinced followers of the free anthroposophical spirit.

In many lectures Rudolf Steiner examined the Whitsun event time and again from many different angles. It is and will be inevitable that in my comments I will be making reference to statements of Rudolf

Steiner. But I would also like to try, as stated in the lecture title, to go quite concretely into the very first Whitsun in the history of mankind, and in order subsequently to clarify its 'connection with Anthroposophy' investigate it fully by means of spiritual science.

First of all I would like to make several digressions.

The first thing I shall be looking at is the question of the pre-Christian background to the Feast of Whitsun. Is Whitsun a new, a Christian feast? Why is it that Whitsun took place exactly on this particular day?

The second digression I wish to make is the consideration of the Feast of Whitsun in relation to the events preceding it. The Whitsun event cannot only be looked at as something in itself. Unlike any other feast it stands in a particular relationship with the events of Easter. Rudolf Steiner also placed it once in the context of a six-monthly period: Christmas, Easter, Whitsun. This therefore is the other matter we want to be looking at this evening: the connections between the feast days, especially Easter, Ascension and finally Whitsun.

First therefore a few words to the origins of the Feast of Whitsun. The Christian Feast of Whitsun has a definite pre-Christian background. It emerged directly from a Jewish ritual. In order to be able to comprehend this we will first cast a look back at the Jewish Feast of Passover, at *Pesach*, from which Good Friday, Easter Saturday and Easter Sunday also emerged. *Pesach,* which begins on the day of the Crucifixion, is the feast in memory of the exodus from Egypt, on which the doors of the Jews were marked with the blood of a lamb as a sign of salvation from slavery. (You see here as well the correspondence with Good Friday, on which the Lamb of God shed His blood for the salvation of mankind.) *Pesach,* however, is also an agricultural festival, a festival of preparation for the harvest of the grain, which by the time of *Pesach* should be sprouting. At that time March was the time for sowing and at *Pesach*, two to three weeks later, the newly sprouted grain was celebrated. After exactly seven weeks had passed, in other words after forty-nine days, the harvest was brought in and a harvest festival celebrated. It was the first wheat harvest of the year. The Hebrew word for sheath is *omer.* The first sheath, which was brought in seven weeks after *Pesach*, was to be offered in the temple. That is why the seven weeks after Pesach are called the 'Counting of the Omer'—the weeks were counted until the harvest of the sheath. This harvest festival, the Jewish Whitsun, is called the 'Festival of Weeks' or *Shavu'ot* (this means 'the weeks', while the word for 'week', *shavua*, is formed from the numeral *shiva*, which means 'seven').

The Counting of the Omer was begun on the second *seder* evening. *Seder* is the traditional meal of the *Pesach* festival, which is always eaten on the evening before each of the days of the festival. The day begins, from an occult perspective, at sunset, in other words in the evening. This means you did not count: Friday, Saturday, Sunday, but you counted Friday evening (= evening before *Shabbat*) and Saturday evening (= evening before Easter Sunday). The second *seder* evening therefore is the start of the Counting of the Omer and fell on Easter Sunday. The actual *Shavu'ot*, and also therefore the Whitsun festival occurs at the end of the forty-nine days, which in exact terms means between Whit Sunday and Whit Monday. In Jewish tradition as well *Shavu'ot* is so closely connected with *Pesach,* that it is often referred to in the Rabbinical literature as *Atzeret,* which means 'completion'.

If we take a look at the relation between both festivals in Christian terms, it can be said that in fact Whitsun is the completion of Easter, the completion of Christ's mission on the Earth. Not just at the time of Christ does Whitsun form this completion of Easter, but the word *Atzeret* is pointing just as much to the future: when the sheath has been brought in, when the spirit of Whitsun has become alive in human beings, only then is completed the spiritual development of the human on Earth, which became possible through the Easter event.

In the diaspora *Schavu'ot* had to lose its character of a harvest festival. Its present-day character is based almost entirely on its second meaning, namely the commemoration of the revelation on Sinai, the giving of the Mosaic tablets of the law.

Shavu'ot and the *Omer*-time were at one time the happiest weeks of the year. But since the destruction of the temple and particularly since the Middle Ages, the *Omer*-time has become a time of mourning, because especially at this time many Jews were persecuted and murdered. *Shavu'ot* itself, however, has remained a joyous festival. In former times the temple, the houses and apartments, the streets, the whole town, were richly decorated with greenery and flowers to the extent they were available. Nowadays the synagogue is still decorated with flowers.

I have often mentioned in the previous lectures that the Christian feast days are almost without exception based on the Jewish feast days and that Christ added a new form of understanding to the old significance of the feasts. The people living at the time of Christ knew nothing else other than these festivals. Their lives were connected with these festival traditions in a way that we today are hardly able to imagine—their whole way of life was arranged around the religious and natural course of the year. And so the old or outer sense of these festivals was used by Christ as a basis of understanding for a new awareness.

Imaginatively, therefore, we can equate the *Feast of Pesach,* which also symbolizes the sprouting process of the seed, with the Easter event. Seven momentous weeks then go by. How the harvest will turn out depends totally on what happens within these weeks. And only he who cultivates his field and knows how to harvest is able to offer the sheaf of corn in the temple of God. This is also clear in the Christian Mystery: on this day the human being can carry his first sheaf of corn into his temple. Understood in the Christian sense the temple is the etheric and physical human body renewed through the Mystery of the Resurrection. Christ said: 'Destroy this temple, and in three days I will raise it up. [...] But he spake of the temple of his body' (John 2:19 f). The human being will carry his sheaf of corn, his harvest into this temple. Only someone who permeates himself with the Easter event, who sows the seed on this Easter day, can receive the harvest of the spirit at Whitsun seven weeks later. Here the spirit can enter into the body. Since the Mystery of Golgotha the harvest festival no longer applies only to the fruits of the Earth but to the fruits of the spirit of the human beings on the Earth.

As I have already pointed out, *Shavu'ot* is also the day on which the revelation on Mount Sinai is celebrated. On this day, alongside the offering of the bread, the pre-Christian ritual is totally devoted to paying homage to the Mosaic law, with commemorating the tablets of the law. The Christian Whitsun festival, in order to be a continuation, a completion of the spirit of the Cross and the Resurrection, has to go beyond this law precisely on this day of Whitsun. We have already mentioned in the lectures—in connection with the Transfiguration on Mount Tabor—how the human being became free from the law through the Christ impulse by being able to follow the spiritual world freely. At the Transfiguration we recognized Moses and Elijah as heralds of the impulse to selfhood, as leaders preparing the way for that which should come through Christ. We recognized Moses as the one who brought the tablets of the law so that the people would remain true to an imageless God, a God of spirit. And finally we recognized Elijah or John the Baptist, who proclaimed what was to come as Christ entered into Jesus of Nazareth: 'He [the new] must increase, but I [the old, who only points to Him] must decrease' (John 3:30).

Because of the laws which fixed humans into a group soul, no individual human self needed to make a personally responsible, moral decision. These laws had to be overcome just as the process of dissolving the ties based on the bloodline was initiated by the flowing of the blood on the Cross. At Whitsun the spirit prevails of a community or of a humanity based on the will of free individuals.

In the verses of the *Calendar of the Soul* which, particularly within the seven weeks between Easter and Whitsun, are built up one after the other in a consistent sequence, you find this process of freeing oneself from the bonds of 'the inner power of narrow selfhood'. The fiftieth day is Whitsun. In Jewish occultism the number 50 is considered to be the outcome of the masculine and feminine principles, represented by the number 1 (Father) and the number 4 (Mother). The future arises, the child, the number 5, when this Chymical Wedding is consummated. The number 50 results when the 5 is multiplied by 10. In the Hebrew alphabet the number 10 is at the same time the letter 'i' or 'j' and means 'God', and in fact that God who is seen as the origin of all existence before everything came into existence; in other words the spirit itself.

And so we find the principle of the Trinity woven out of the archetypal cosmos (Father, the number 1), Earth (Mother, the number 4) and the cosmos of the future (Child, the number 5). And the Feast of Whitsun can be realized as the birth of the Christ Spirit in those human souls who are aware that this principle of the Trinity is the point of emergence of cosmic existence and the culminating point for the evolution of the cosmos.

This a very abbreviated description. But at least some indication has been given of how the Feast of Whitsun arose out of ancient Jewish ritual.

Before I now come to the historical description of the first Feast of Whitsun I wish to make a second short digression.

We were only just speaking about the Trinity which, for those who recognize it, speaks out of the Feast of Whitsun. What does this feast have to do with the Trinity? Of course the Trinity existed before the Feast of Whitsun was celebrated for the first time. The difference is simply that through the events directly proceeding from this first Whitsun, every human being on the Earth is able to know the Trinity. Previously the ancient initiates had an understanding of this secret, but firstly they were always looking up towards this cosmic truth as it shone down on the Earth from beyond the Earth, and secondly, they could only perceive this truth in the out-of-the-body state lasting three-and-a-half days of ancient initiation.

But now the circumstances had changed. With the completion of Christ's mission every human being was given the possibility of comprehending the Trinity without having to leave his body.

The mission of Christ, the plan of the Gods, encompassed the festivals of Christmas, Easter, and Whitsun. On Christmas Day the body was prepared into which the Father God could send His Son. The power of the Father God is expressed in this event: *Ex deo nascimur*. Since then the human being can feel that he as well is born out of the immense Godhead and into his earthly body.

There then follows the Easter festival, in which the human being can know the Son of God while on Earth. The human being has to become aware that of course he inhabits a body but he is not just a body. The human being can understand that in death his soul can rise again in Christ: *In Christo morimur*.

Rudolf Steiner once said: 'From the moment of this inner experience of Easter, if we now suffuse the spirit which has become centred within itself with meaning that is not from this world but from the spiritual world, we will experience Whitsun. It depends on this inner experience of Easter whether we experience Whitsun' (GA 118, 15 May 1910). This is why Whitsun is firmly linked to the movable feast of Easter.

Putting it into one simple sentence: the Father sends the Son who brings tidings of the Holy Spirit.

These are the three parts of the half-yearly period: Christmas, Easter, Whitsun. And we can refer again to the diagram from the last lecture and change it somewhat to indicate what we mean:

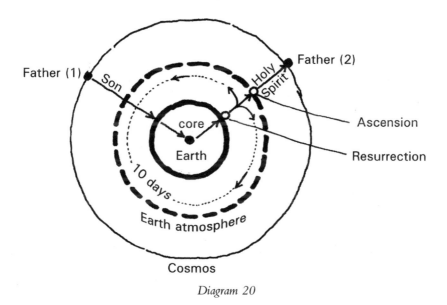

Diagram 20

The Father sends the Son to the Earth. The Son experiences earthly death, He penetrates the body of the Earth, and the Resurrection takes place. From now on, through the Holy Spirit, the human being is able to bring about the return to the Father.

This is the basis for understanding karma. You can only understand the idea of karma when you have first come to an understanding of the idea of Whitsun, for Whitsun is not a 'passive' festival of grace like Easter, for which the human being must do nothing, Whitsun is rather a festival where the human being is active. Here the human being can work positively on his karma if the Rosicrucian saying lives within him. He knows that he is at home in the spiritual world: *Per spiritum sanctum reviviscimus. Reviviscimus* means, we will live again. The human being must take this step himself within evolution on the Earth: the fully conscious step of returning to the Father, developing himself through all his incarnations. The possibility of taking this step has been given to him by the Son of God ('No one cometh unto the Father, but by me'—John 14:6). But it is up to the human being to carry it out.

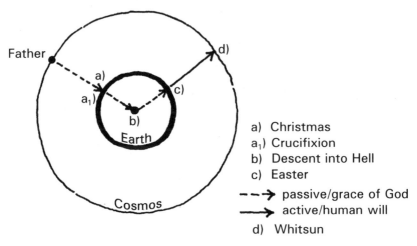

a) Christmas
a₁) Crucifixion
b) Descent into Hell
c) Easter
- - -> passive/grace of God
——> active/human will
d) Whitsun

Diagram 21

I would now like to talk about the historical facts and amplify them immediately with an explanation according to spiritual science, so that the contemplation of these historic days does not get stuck in externals. As I have so often mentioned, inner facts penetrate the outer ones and vice versa.

First though I would like to start with the events of the Ascension. It is extremely important that this event also be considered from the standpoint of spiritual science, and we want to look at it in order, as well, to be able to understand Whitsun better. On Ascension Day further conditions for Whitsun were created.

When we speak about the Ascension we are obliged to bear in mind that on Ascension Day, as at other times before, the disciples did not see Christ with physical eyes when they perceived Him in His Resurrection body, but they saw him—as Rudolf Steiner says—with *eyes of the soul* (GA 224, 7 May 1923).

In the early morning darkness on Ascension Day, Christ and the disciples left the house of the Last Supper. Christ taught until sunrise and then they took the road to Gethsemane. The women also came, as well as a few other disciples. He radiated all the love that can ever possibly be given on the Earth. They climbed the Mount of Olives together, Christ almost weightless and moving faster and faster, so that the disciples could hardly follow Him. Similar to several older depictions of the event a rainbow, coming from another sphere, appeared around Him. He then became brighter than the Sun, which was just rising behind the Mount of Olives—He was Himself the Sun, He became the Sun. Before it became impossible to make Him out in this extremely bright Sun-like radiance, He gave the Earth His blessing by raising His left arm as though He were letting the power of the cosmos flow into Him, and out into the Earth through His right arm which pointed down to the ground. By placing His left hand on His chest, on His heart, He then sent this stream out to mankind through His right hand, which made a sign of blessing. It was an indescribable stream of cosmic love which sent the whole superhuman love of Christ out from its home in the stars to the Earth by flowing out of the cosmos through the left hand into the heart, and streaming out of the heart through the right hand to the Earth. So it appeared as though the resurrected Son of God was binding—by raising his left hand to the heavens and holding His right hand down to the Earth—the macrocosmos and the microcosmos together through an eternal divine bond of unqualified devotion and self-sacrificing love. (The statue of Christ by Rudolf Steiner and Edith Maryon manifests this.)

Understanding the actual event of the Ascension is based on the knowledge of the Resurrection body and its relationship to the sphere surrounding the Earth.

The form in which the physical forces of Christ, which since the Resurrection had appeared again and again to the disciples, is not a body of flesh and blood, but a spirit body perceptible to the eyes of the soul of the disciples and the women who had been prepared to perceive it. This Resurrection body or the so-called phantom was 'the archetype' or 'the real idea of the physical body existing in the external world, with all the attributes of the physical body' (GA 131, 10 October 1911), as Rudolf Steiner expresses it. You can easily recognize the subtle difference in the Resurrection body to a physical, material earthly body or to a pure spirit, as Christ in His Resurrection body performed all sorts of physical movements. He also climbed up the Mount of Olives ahead of the disciples. He did not float in the air.

However, neither did he have the typical heaviness of the Earth about Him; He was simply not bound by the laws of the material Earth.

To a certain extent this phantom body still existed as an outer form in the world up until the Ascension; it alone was the seat of the Christ Spirit after the Resurrection. For the disciples it was perceptible as the individuality of the Saviour, outwardly influencing them from the soul and spirit sphere. Even after the Resurrection, Christ taught the disciples time and again in and through this Resurrection body.

But then, after thirty-nine days, the time had come for this phantom to proceed to its actual place of purpose. I have already pointed out repeatedly in previous lectures that a set of laws prevail for Christ which are inverse to those for normal earthly humans, as Rudolf Steiner mentions in his lectures on the *Fifth Gospel* (GA 148). The Baptism can be seen as the conception of Christ. The three years in the body of Jesus is the time of growth for Christ, and while the human being is born into earthly life Christ is born into earthly death, which means that the death of Jesus is the birth of Christ. And the place where Christ actually lives has already been described, namely in the body of the Earth, which becomes His physical body between the death on the Cross of Jesus of Nazareth and the Resurrection, within the thirty-nine hours which lie between. We can take another glance at our diagram—this life unfolds within the spiritual and physical spheres of the body of the Earth (see diagram 20, p. 153: 'Journey through the Earth—descent and ascent').

But I ask you now to understand what I will be saying entirely within the context just explained. The Resurrection is actually the death of Christ. As the Resurrection body rises from the earthly grave, Christ crosses over the threshold and—in the unique manner we have been made familiar with—He overcomes death for mankind, He renders death immortal. (This does not mean that death will never cease, rather death no longer has to be died in the old sense anymore.) That is why deep wisdom lies in the words of *The Foundation Stone Meditation*: 'In Christ death becomes life'. Christ is in this living death in the Resurrection body with human beings for thirty-nine days, in other words between Easter and Ascension. He can be experienced and is visible to the strengthened eyes of the soul of the disciples and the women. But if now Christ's crossing of the threshold, His passing through the 'Gates of Death', is the Resurrection, what then is the Ascension? After the passage of these thirty-nine days the Christ Spirit merges in this unique phantom body, the second Adam, into the sphere which can be called 'Devachan' according to the context just explained. There He is invisible to the eyes of the disciples, He disappears from their vision, in front of the eyes of their soul He merges into this sphere. The entry of the phantom body into this devachanic sphere is the Ascension. This devachanic sphere of Christ is the sphere surrounding the Earth. According to our diagram you can take the saying of Christ literally: 'No one cometh to the Father except by me' (John 14:16; see diagram 20, p. 153). Through the area marked by the broken line, through the etheric sphere surrounding the Earth inhabited by Christ, the human being must pass if he wishes to come to the Father. What the Christ Spirit is able to stream into him, if he will only allow it to stream into him, he must use to begin the journey to the Father based on a conscious and firm decision.

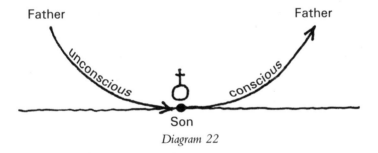

Diagram 22

Rudolf Steiner describes in his Whitsun lecture from 15 May 1910 this event of the Ascension in the following way (GA 118): 'In the so-called Ascension, the bodily form which the founder of Christianity had assumed after the Mystery of Golgotha was dissolved in a powerful vision perceptible to his nearest followers'. Rudolf Steiner in fact only developed the concept of the phantom one year later (cf. *From Jesus to Christ*, GA 131), but you notice from the sentence how an awareness of it is already forming.

The disciples beheld, therefore, how Christ in His phantom body dissolved as it were and merged into the cosmic sphere surrounding the Earth. This is Christ in the etheric realm, whom more and more humans today and in the future are and will be able to see—this means the human being can have more capabilities today than the disciples, who at that time could indeed see the phantom in its bodily form on the Earth, but not Christ in the etheric. Only Paul was capable of that.

For the disciples the Ascension was a powerful and radical vision. The light of the cosmos, of the pure spirit which is not of this world, united with the radiance of the light of the Resurrection body, which shone as brightly as on the Easter morning—only this time the disciples and the women were aware of it. And so it appeared as though His Resurrection body dissolved in the fusion of these two sources of light. It was as though two fires joined together into the light of one powerful flame. The Sun rose behind Him and from behind the Mount of Olives. He shone brighter than the Sun though. And as His head and face were the first to turn into a Sun and merge with the Father Sun and only then His body (just as the head is also the most perfect part of the human body), so that His feet were the last to merge into the all-embracing radiance, it was as though he ascended into heaven. You often find this naively portrayed in old paintings by a pair of feet looking out from the underside of a sun or shining cloud.

Because the light was brighter than the Sun all those present fell to the ground, and as the Christ Being had immersed itself into the sphere surrounding the Earth the disciples became aware of two spiritual beings who promised them that Christ would return. Nevertheless the disciples felt as though something had been taken away from them and in the days that followed they turned to the Mother of Jesus for support and to the prayer they said in the house of the Last Supper as protection against the high priests.

There now follow a further ten days between Ascension and Whitsun. What happened in these ten days? Something decisive happened on the Earth and something else, just as decisive, happened in the heavens.

On the Earth these ten days go by, but their unique significance is at first only for the disciples and the women. These individuals who had accompanied Christ went through a particular process in these ten days. Even the number of days has a special meaning. Why do exactly ten days go by between Ascension and Whitsun? *One* occult reason is that the ten days are the days of the Christ impulse, in the same way the Ten Commandments are the Ten Commandments of Moses. We are reminded of what was said previously: *Shavu'ot* is also the festival of the tablets of the law, the honouring of the Ten Commandments.

Now, however, in these ten days and up to the ancient *Shavu'ot* festival, the development of the disciples had to move away completely from the laws of Moses, and away from that which bound them as members of an ethnic group to this law: the bloodline. Otherwise they would not have been able to apply consciously the freedom they had won at Easter to receiving the spirit. The old covenant created dependency and had to be overcome. This does not affect the integrity of the Ten Commandments. It is only that after Christ, the individual self ought not to relinquish its individual moral responsibility to a law.

In these ten days the compulsion which subjected a group, a community, to the divine law of the Ten Commandments had to be overcome. The disciples had to get away completely from everything connected with the bloodline. Even the phantom, which was still visible until the Ascension event as the form of the physical body, had to disappear. They had to separate themselves totally from the idea that Christ could only appear to them clothed in the one form in which He had encountered them. A new era could only begin when the phantom had been dissolved. But this also had to be spurred on actively by the hearts of the disciples in these ten days.

Within these ten days they also had to come to understand that the phantom had not dissolved into nothing. What happened on Ascension Day and the days that followed can be roughly compared to the way salt completely dissolves in a liquid and the liquid retains the presence, the taste of the salt. Not just the Christ Spirit and those parts of the etheric body, which we can term the etherically transformed blood from the stigmata which flowed from the Cross, merged into the etheric sphere of the Earth, but the Resurrection body of Christ finally merged into it as well on Ascension Day. Here we are dealing with cosmic alchemy. The spiritual substance of the phantom body, and I beg you not to understand this in a material sense, the spiritual substance of the Resurrection body was denser than the substance of the Earth's etheric sphere, in the same way that the salt crystal is denser than water and yet is still able to dissolve in water. A new liquid is created—the Earth is sheathed in a new etheric mantle.

The disciples understood more and more clearly that the Mosaic laws cannot shape the future path, and that a relationship with the Godhead can only arise out of an inner fire of longing for the spirit.

Having developed a feeling for how Christ had saved the human etheric and physical bodies from decline by His deed on Golgotha, they had become aware of this from their perception of the phantom body; the disciples then felt the need for the soul and the spirit! They longed of their own accord for the new fulfilment this living body could bring, they longed with all their strength for the renewal of the astral body and the self. So strong was their longing that after the Ascension many of them became sad, because what they had had from without, from Christ in the Resurrection body, no longer gave them fulfilment. They came to see, however, that the phantom which appeared to their souls, so harmonious and divine, in which inner and outer aspects corresponded in the most wonderful harmony—that this archetype had passed over from the visible Earth into the invisible sphere surrounding the Earth but was able now and in the future to enter into every human being and first of all into each one of them. They recognized here what the actual Christ impulse meant. Now they could finally experience Whitsun.

The other phenomenon which occurred within these ten days and not on the Earth but in the Heavens was that the first phantom, the first Resurrection body of Christ, which had ascended on Ascension Day, began to replicate itself in the cosmic ether of the Earth, like the process of salt dissolving in a liquid which results in the dissolved salt permeating the liquid completely. In each drop of the liquid a part of the salt is to be found. And so Christ prepared Himself to enter into those individuals who in truth are seriously striving and thirsting. This is a cosmic process that is so powerful, in its significance for the future evolution of mankind as well, that we would have to devote a whole lecture to it. You can find references to it in Rudolf Steiner's lecture cycle *From Jesus to Christ*.

In these ten days the understanding grew in the disciples that the phantom had to go to its place of purpose so that Christ can fully accomplish His deed. The completion (*Atzeret*) of the Gods' plan lay in the Feast of Whitsun. The tongues of flame which were bestowed on each one of them are also a symbol for the seed of the phantom body. In these ten days the first Resurrection body replicated itself and on the tenth day it was possible, for the first time in the entire evolution of the Earth, for a human being to put on this seed of the phantom body, this 'drop of salt water' meant specifically for him.

We can again refer to Rudolf Steiner's diagram with a few small additions of our own:

Development 1

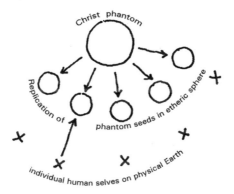

Development 2

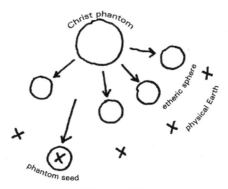

Diagram 23

We now want to turn to the event of Whitsun which actually took place in the night from Sunday to Monday—at dawn on the Monday.

As we have already established for the other festivals connected with the Mystery of Golgotha, Whitsun also had an effect on outer events, although it constitutes at the same time an occult event. The esoteric background to the Feast of Whitsun also has exoteric effects. When mention is made of the 'sound of the rushing of a mighty wind' then this is to be understood esoterically and exoterically.

Seen esoterically this mighty rushing sound, of which the Acts of the Apostles speaks, means that the souls of the disciples were raised to a higher level of vision.

As the fire spirit came over them they had a vision of the future evolution of humanity, namely that they would carry this fire impulse into their next incarnation. They felt that what the human being had once acquired does not get lost in succeeding incarnations.

For many of the visitors to Jerusalem who were camping on the surrounding hills and also in the city between Easter and Whitsun—they were there because of the Jewish holidays—a rushing storm-like sound was actually perceptible. Those who, since Easter and from the time before, looked upon the events surrounding Jesus of Nazareth with good will, even perceived a cloud of light which formed over the house of the Last Supper. They had already developed more powers of perception than the others. This cloud of light and fire sank down, penetrating even the ceiling of the room in which the disciples and the women were staying. It was first of all like the spirit which descended at the Baptism, only many times more powerful, immense and roaring. This living cloud hung for a while over the city district of Zion, over the house, over the room, over the disciples. Then it was as if the cloud broke—as if the one decisive moment had come when the decision was made for it to fragment. It sent many single rays of light and fire out from itself which poured over those present and penetrated into every single one of them. Visible at the centre and simultaneously around this cloud of fire was again a rainbow whose ends were touching, closing together as though forming a circle in space. It was like a gate that opened to a reality which otherwise existed hidden and invisible behind a cosmic wall, behind the veil of the sensory world, and which now became visible through this gate. The spirit of Heaven passed through this gate and into the human beings on Earth. Those present perceived, felt this in the exalted state of an incipient new initiation, and it was as though they thirsted after this light of the fire. Their thirst for this spiritual fire was actually the decisive factor at this Whitsun event, because the spirit entered individually into each one in the same intensity and quality as their thirst.

A few spirit fires resembled some essential parts of the rainbow, others were more extensive and even more like the fiery source. It is like the Grail feast where every one receives the food he desires. The meal was individually 'tailor-made' for each person.

It was a powerful imagination of tremendous significance for the understanding of the disciples! For each one had *his* flame, was suffused by his own flame and at the same time perceived the flames, in other words the spirit, as it penetrated the others. It was extremely important that the disciples looked at one another in this way, actually mutually recognized one another. They comprehended the other for the first time as a unique and individual self, different from them, through whom the spirit acts and shines. For the first time they knew that the Holy Spirit is in the other person as well, and speaks in its entirety through these other people—sounds different through these people as through me and speaks as one and the same spirit out of him and out of me. The other person can manifest in his own particular way the same spirit, for the tongues of fire he carries over his head, in his breast and in his mouth, spring from the same source.

This way the disciples knew with certainty: I and the other person are individuals, but we are both united with one another and with the other fire-bearers; we are perfectly at one through the immense unifying power of the Sun, which is now to be found on the Earth. Everything in us strives towards the One and this unites us in truth. It is no longer the blood which welds us together, but this source of the spirit, the universal, divine and single source of human selfhood.

In this way there arose a new community, that which Rudolf Steiner calls the 'community of brothers' (cf. for example, the lecture from 29 June 1908 in GA 104). This community of brothers was born at the time of Christ and is the community of the future, which is able to withstand the counter impulse which has arisen and will arise through the individualization of human beings: egoism, materialism. The disciples realized that this community exists through the fact that after the Ascension the Christ Spirit had united with the Father Spirit and was now to be found poured out into their souls, which were longing for Christ. So they understood what it meant when Christ said to them: 'I am with you always even unto the end of the world' (Matthew 28:20). He was with them and was in fact in every indi-

vidual self, no longer outside and to a certain extent isolated from
them as a divine individuality in an outer form, but *in* mankind. That is
why the outer Christ had to disappear, why the phantom had to merge
into the surrounding etheric sphere so that as a seed He could enter
into those humans who longed for these seeds, and as a result return to
Earth. In this way the deed of the Gods was completed. The
knowledge of the Trinity had flowed into the awareness of humans on
the Earth. Christmas: Father; Easter: Son; Whitsun: Holy Spirit. As a
result the Trinity, which previously only the ancient initiates were able
to behold, had descended to Earth, so that all mankind could become
aware of it as a reality active on the Earth.

As a supplement to our investigation of the events of the Ascension
and of Whitsun we can draw on the following explanation from
Rudolf Steiner:

> Only after the unified bodily nature [this is the phantom!] of Christ
> has merged as a unity into the spiritual nature of the Earth, does the
> possibility exist for the hearts of those who understood the Christ
> impulse to be able to speak about this Christ impulse, to be active in
> the spirit of this Christ impulse. The Christ impulse submerged
> itself, to the extent it was manifested in outer bodily forms, into the
> unity of the spiritual world through the Ascension; ten days later it
> reappeared again in the hearts of single individuals, of those who
> were the first to understand (GA 118, 15 May 1910).

The human being, therefore, is able to feel two things at Whitsun:
individualization and the resulting coming together freely with all
human souls.

With the understanding we now have of the nature of the phantom
from before and after the Ascension, we can approach the secret of
Whitsun once again from another angle. There are an endless number
of perspectives from which we can look at this Mystery event. We can
even look at it in physical and mathematical terms: at the place where
Christ goes to after the Resurrection, space does not exist. Coming
from the Sun, Christ, the bringer of time, carries this Sun into the
Earth. In the place from which time comes, however, time is not as it
is for us, because it has no space to overcome. Space as we know it
does not exist. Seen from our perspective, time there runs backwards.

You experience this every night when in sleep you enter the spiritual world, or after death, when you first live through your experiences on Earth in reverse. If you encounter a spiritual entity beyond the threshold, then it is not as though you approach it, but as though it approaches you from the depths of the spiritual being of time.

Now Christ, the Sun-Time Being, has through His connection with the Earth brought His time to the Earth. In the Mystery of Golgotha, therefore, you have a certain interpenetration of both principles of space and time. Subject to the laws of the Earth, conceived, incarnated and died, the divine being wanders through space. However, this God carries His cosmic time, the backwards flowing, spaceless time, with Him in all these processes. That is why that happens which I have mentioned previously: the inversion of the 'sequence of events' in Christ's life.

The phantom body now merges through the Ascension into the sphere surrounding the Earth, where it replicates itself. Here lies an important and wondrous Mystery, because for the first time through the passage of God through earthly, material death and through the subsequent Resurrection, the spiritual archetype of the *physical* body was able to overcome this death, this imprisonment in space. You could say: the spiritual essence of this physical human body was able to merge into cosmic time from the dimension of space, just as the salt crystal merges into a liquid. As a result, the spiritual expression of the physical body became free. It was the counter image to the old, the first Adam, which became embedded into space as it sank down to the Earth. This is why Paul speaks especially of the 'second' or 'new' Adam, as he was aware precisely of this difference (1 Corinthians 15:45–49; Romans 5:14).

And as this first phantom, at the Ascension, which we have also described as the death of Christ, as the crossing of the threshold, as in other words this phantom returned to the reversed, cosmic time—and this time not as a pure divine spirit, but as a *physical* imprint, which He had been able to attain by means of the process of incarnation—the foundation was laid for Christ to become the Lord of Karma. For the human being can only assume responsibility towards his future incarnations through the fact that after death he does not remain a captive in space but passes into cosmic time. For after death he will now be going backwards through the life he has just cast off and working on it afterwards in the spiritual world with a sense of moral responsibility, so that he will be fully prepared for his next life.

The first feast of Whitsun occurred as finally, after ten days, the disciples had perceived that they could realize this Mystery if they themselves would develop, would 'put on' like a garment, such a replicated phantom. They foresaw that the human being could in this way become immortal, and that the spirit of Whitsun, that flared up in each one of them, was the highest expression of individuality. It was the expression of an individuality which, when it had put itself in the 'right relationship with Christ', could come, through the course of time, to resemble more and more the phantom of Christ. Solely by means of his incarnations on Earth, by becoming flesh time and again, can the human being approach Christ in His Resurrection body.

As the sound of roaring died down, an infinite trust and assurance passed into the disciples and the women. They felt they were absolutely pulsating with this fire, which had become their own. This was the baptism with the fire of the Holy Spirit through Christ in the supersensible world. The disciples baptized with water, but they themselves were not baptized with water, they received the baptism of fire.

The light was perceived by many who during the life of Jesus were His followers and from those who after the Crucifixion and after the Resurrection had come to believe. They pushed towards the house of the Last Supper in order to discover what had taken place. The others, however, became even more hardened, even more inflexible towards the revelation of the light of love, by the presence of the spirit in those who thirsted after Christ.

Many people had gathered there and that is why Simon Peter and John, who worked mostly together after the departure of Christ, went out to speak to them. Simon Peter turned to the people. You can read his speech, his fiery awakening call, in the Acts of the Apostles (Acts 2). For the first time in public he announced that God had raised Jesus of Nazareth, that Christ had been incarnated in this man and that this being had been nailed to the Cross. After that, Peter preached that the baptism, the conception of the Holy Spirit, would unite mankind into a new covenant.

What Simon Peter had spoken passed directly into the enlightened people. They understood him as if he were speaking in their own language. This does not mean that people from all the countries of the world with the most diverse languages were present, but that what Peter had said appeared to each person to have been formulated solely for his own individual understanding. They were able to be spoken to in a state of higher awareness in which earthly language is superfluous. The spirit of fire which spoke out of Peter penetrated into the innermost core of each enlightened person.

Peter subsequently instructed several of the disciples to perform baptism. Afterwards the mother of Jesus blessed these disciples as though she were their own mother.

On the evening before the Ascension the disciples were taught many things by Christ about the act of baptism and its ritual performance. And so the disciples had already made advance arrangements. A house of teaching at the pool where the baptisms were to take place had been decorated festively and there they took the water blessed by Christ in a waterskin, as well as a delicately-formed palm leaf Christ had chosen for the ceremony. They also took a square-shaped lump of salt with them which was to be dissolved in the holy water.

The pool lay in the valley to the east of Zion, in other words between Zion in the West, the city district where the poor lived in the East and bordered in the North by the steep slope at the southern wall of the temple. It was a natural pool and the bottom was not bricked or tiled over like the Pool of Siloah. It was surrounded by five amphitheatre-like terraces. It was fed by several streams as well as by its own spring. On the day of *Pesach* the streams also carried the blood of the offerings from the temple into the pool.

The ceremony of baptism stretched over the whole day. First Simon and John blessed the pool by sprinkling the holy water over the pool with the palm leaf. John then threw the lump of salt into the water and everyone remained for a moment of dignified silence in contemplation of the occult process in which the 'salt of the Earth' dissolved in the waters of the pool (the watery element corresponds, when understood esoterically, to the etheric of the Earth). They were reminded of the occult process of the phantom dissolving into the etheric sphere around the Earth.

Simon had a chair for teaching on a raised spot next to the pool from which now and again he gave a speech. Each candidate for baptism received a white baptismal robe from the women before the baptism, as a sign that he was allowing the spirit to enter into a new and purified house. The garments, like the robes of the temple servants, possessed black ribbons at the neck, which in the temple were normally worn tied together as a reminder of subjection to the Mosaic Law. Even today orthodox Jews tie on the so-called *tefillin* when praying, which fulfils a similar function. The black ribbons were untied after the baptism as a sign that this subjection has been overcome, as a sign of the new covenant. The confession of faith in God was now to be made in freedom and not in subjection.

At the five entrances to the pool the disciples now baptized with the help of clay basins. The candidates for baptism were not submerged under water as John the Baptist had done, but in fact it was a baptism by water full of symbolism intended to bring to mind the principle of the Trinity. That is why water was poured with the hand over the head of the candidate three times. The ones who had been baptized first held their hands over the heads of the newly baptized as though they wished to bear witness to the holy event or become Godparents.

The ancient *Shavu'ot* festival received new meaning. The spiritual seed had germinated in those who since Easter had been touched by the Mystery of Christ.

Question: 'How did the high priests behave on this day?'

According to tradition an offering of a 'sheaf of corn' was also made by the disciples, John and Simon Peter, as was the custom, bringing an offering of two loaves to the temple. Whole mountains of loaves were piled up as thousands of people had brought their bread there. One of the two loaves would be a burnt offering, the other was meant for the poor. The high priests were totally busy the whole day with organizing this harvest festival and honouring the holy tablets of the law. In their duties they seemed to have mentally cut themselves off from the spiritual baptism at the pool. It was as though on this day they did not want to know anything about it. They anyway could not have organized anything against the teaching and baptism, as on this day many hundreds of people had come to the pool and the atmosphere there was very euphoric and later as well in the temple district, because many of those who had been baptized brought their offerings of bread to the temple. The first day of the baptism ended on a sad note though, with the temporary arrest of Simon Peter and John. After they had passed through the inner area of the temple with their bread, they were arrested on the instructions of Caiaphas for rabble-rousing.

Let us now return for a moment to the proper Whitsun mood. We are able to establish that the Feast of Whitsun is characterized by two elements: by the awareness of a community which can only arise through the individualization of the human self and its striving towards the spirit. The human celebrates a new kind of covenant. He celebrates the free merging together of all human souls by loving them as individuals.

When we celebrate Whitsun we realize that in comparison to Easter nothing simply 'happens' at Whitsun in the way that we can wait for the Crucifixion on Good Friday or for the Resurrection on Easter Sunday. Whitsun is not the day on which something happens to the human being by divine grace, whether he will or not. The human being celebrates Whitsun when he is ready to relate to the Mystery of Golgotha in the spirit of Christ. He *himself* must be active for Whitsun to happen. The disciples had to develop the longing for the transformation of their souls themselves, so that the spirit could enter into them. After Christ's deed the disciples wanted to bestow on their transformed and living physical and etheric bodies an appropriately transformed and living inner being.

By means of the Feast of Whitsun the human being therefore comes on the one hand to an understanding of the most sublime selfhood. But at the same time he gives himself freely and selflessly—in other words, in selfhood, not in egoism—to the brotherhood of man; he strives in freedom towards a community of all souls.

Also we can recognize that whoever experiences the power of the cosmic spirit needs no earthly language. He realizes his unity with *every* human soul, even when it belongs to a different culture and speaks so strangely. The Holy Spirit from Whitsun enables all individuals to understand one another. This is the reason for the image of the disciples speaking in all the languages of the Earth.

The neophytes in the Whitsun mystery inwardly follow these two paths.

The most prominent aspect of Whitsun, however, is its connection to the present and to the future. From the very first feast of Whitsun the Christ impulse was no longer proclaimed by Christ Himself, but by the spirit, by the hearts and mouths of men. And this is the case for today and for the future.

Rudolf Steiner says something decisive in his lecture cycle GA 118 about this aspect:

> The Christ impulse, however, is an impulse of freedom. The impact, in the truest sense of the word, of this impulse is not shown when it is active outside the human soul. The true impact of the Christ impulse first appears when it is active itself in the individual human soul. And those who were the first to understand Christ felt called upon by what happened at Whitsun to proclaim what was present in their own souls, what was revealed to them as the teachings of Christ in the revelations and inspirations of their own souls. [... They felt] called upon by the power of the impulse of Christ active in them to allow the fiery tongues, the individualized Holy Spirit, to speak in them and to go and proclaim Christ. Those who understood the meaning of Whitsun in this way recognized not just simply what Christ had said to them, not just those words which Christ had spoken, but they recognized as words of Christ what comes from the power of a soul which feels the impulse of Christ within. That is why it is an individualized Holy Spirit which pours itself into every single human soul which develops within itself the strength to feel the impulse of Christ (GA 118, 15 May 1910).

Therefore the proclamation of Christ must always sound anew, always different in each epoch in the history of mankind.

The people who did this, however, who spoke according to the spirit of Whitsun, in the spirit of Christ, have been subject at all times to the most awful and infamous attacks and slanders. In the Gospel of John there are already references to be found to this development in what was then still the future. Even Jesus Christ spoke about it (John 15:18)—in my Zurich edition of the Bible under the heading 'Jesus warns the disciples of persecution'—I quote: 'If the world hateth you, you know that it hath hated me before it hated you. If ye were of the world, the world would love its own: but because ye are not of the world, but I chose you out of the world, therefore the world hateth you. [...] But all these things will they do unto to you for my name's sake, because they know not him that sent me. [...] But this cometh to pass, that the word may be fulfilled that is written in their law, They hated me without a cause'.

Of course it was not much different for Rudolf Steiner as for all the others who have proclaimed and defended the impulse of Christ:

> I have often pointed out before that this effect [of the Mystery of Golgotha] takes such a direction. Among others once in a lecture cycle bearing the title *From Jesus to Christ*, which was held in Karlsruhe and which was treated with the utmost hostility, precisely because certain truths, which some people wanted to keep veiled, were spoken of openly out of a sense of esoteric duty. Indeed, one can say, that precisely from this lecture cycle on, the hostility from certain quarters towards Anthroposophy actually first began (GA 224, 7 May 1923).

I am quite sure that accusations will also be laid against me because of these lectures, indeed it has already happened repeatedly—characteristically enough only from those who have not heard the lectures at all. I could foresee straightaway that I would be accused of presumption for holding the lectures, as has already come to my attention. I want to bring this up just this once precisely because Whitsun is the occasion for asking myself whether I will always profess my complete faith in Christ. Whether I will also remain loyal to the Whitsun spirit of Anthroposophy—in the spirit of the fighter for peace, of the Christ impulse, Rudolf Steiner—or let myself be intimidated by accusations of presumption. Something like this is always a very complicated matter, for who would like it if his lectures describing the most precious event in the history of mankind were to be judged as presumptuous?! It is already difficult enough, struggling at each lecture for words that are only halfway appropriate. You really do then consider whether it would be better to say nothing, for the last thing I wish to happen is for any harm to come to the Mystery of Golgotha. But this is basically how a *circulus vitiosus*, a vicious circle, begins. If I were to hide away and no longer speak about these things, this will achieve what a few people want. But in my heart I know that I would deny that which has inspired me to speak. I would deny and conceal Him whom I have to thank for my life, and all that which glows within and all the goodness actually to be found in the soul.

Whoever nowadays also speaks about the Mystery of Golgotha, or even about Christ Himself, is unfortunately always in danger of being made out to be presumptuous, especially if he has not yet achieved old age. This immediately nips any discussion in the bud. A little more open-mindedness and understanding for the other individual self could open the possibilities for communication. But who in fact do we really have to answer to—irrespective of who we are, where we come from, how old we are, what our karma is? We have only to answer to ourselves and to the spiritual world.

But the Christ impulse, Rudolf Steiner says, is 'not a teaching or a doctrine . . . , but a force, which must be experienced in the innermost heart of the soul' (GA 118). If you speak about the impulse of Christ, then this must also be alive as the fire of Whitsun in human beings. Each one of us can measure himself against this standard and answer for himself to the spiritual world.

In his lecture on 15 May 1910, Rudolf Steiner pleaded, in fiery words, for Anthroposophy and its relation to Whitsun. He said: 'We, who know that in the present-day, in spiritual science, we ourselves are proclaiming the words of Christ ringing out to us from the spirit choirs . . . understand the actual meaning of Whitsun. When we feel called upon to constantly gain new wisdom from Christianity, then the wisdom we gain will be precisely that wisdom which is appropriate for the soul evolving from incarnation to incarnation' (GA 118, 15 May 1910).

Also connected with this understanding is Rudolf Steiner's constant summons, almost a plea, to familiarize ourselves as far as is possible in life with the Christ impulse, to undertake the attempt again and again, however often it may fail, to constantly draw new secrets from the Mystery of Golgotha. And by accepting this task in free will, as a need of his own heart, the human being prepares himself for his life after death. Rudolf Steiner said: 'This is why Christ came down to Earth, because the power of the deed of the Mystery of Golgotha had to influence human beings in a physical body. As a result the Christ force can at first only have an influence on humans in a physical body.... But only as much of the Christ impulse as the human being has received in his life, between birth and death, will be brought to perfection by this impulse in him' (GA 118, 15 May 1910).

And in another passage in the same lecture is said: 'Just as the first disciples—each one—received the Christ impulse, were free to receive it as their own soul-inspiring tongues of fire, so could all of you, if you make the effort to understand the impulse of Christ, receive the Christ impulse in your hearts, receive and individualize the forces which will allow you to act in the spirit of this impulse in a more and more perfect way'. This is putting on the phantom.

Since the time of Christ, many people, particularly within the Anthroposophical Society, already have one or two incarnations behind them, incarnations in which they have already made some progress in this work of perfection. We are of course still standing at the beginning of this evolution, but it has already advanced to such a stage that more and more people today are able to have an experience similar to Paul's. More and more people will be having a Damascus experience, in which by means of intensified spiritual forces they will be able to see Christ as He appears in His etheric form, and will as a result possess the same strength of assurance of His presence as Paul possessed then. Upon this strength of assurance and through Anthroposophy, may Whitsun, as Rudolf Steiner once said, be for the whole cosmos!

Acknowledgement

My deepest gratitude goes to Peter Tradowsky, who has been a close and selfless spiritual companion to me. We owe it to his lifelong anthroposophical spiritual work that the first attempts could be made in this book towards a deeper understanding of the phenomena which have occurred and their importance for an understanding of the human being. His attempts can form the background for further individual research.

Judith von Halle
Berlin, August 2005

List of Rudolf Steiner's works quoted in the lectures

English titles of works by Rudolf Steiner are given only in cases where a similar (though not always identical) volume to the original German edition from the collected works—the *Gesamtausgabe* (abbreviated as 'GA')—has been published in English translation. In many cases lectures are available in typescript or in print as single lectures or compilations from the collected works. For information on these, contact Rudolf Steiner House Library, 35 Park Road, London NW1 6XT, or similar anthroposophical libraries around the world.

GA 010   *Knowledge of the Higher Worlds, How is it Achieved?* (1904/05)
GA 013   *Occult Science, An Outline* (1910)
GA 054   *Die Welträtsel und die Anthroposophie*
GA 096   *Ursprungsimpulse der Geisteswissenschaft, Christliche Esoterik im Lichte neuer Geist-Erkenntnis*
GA 097   *The Christian Mystery*
GA 099   *Rosicrucian Wisdom*
GA 103   *The Gospel of St John*
GA 104   *The Apocalypse of St John*
GA 104a *Reading the Pictures of the Apocalypse*
GA 105   *Universe, Earth and Man*
GA 107   *Geisteswissenschaftliche Menschenkunde*
GA 118   *Das Ereignis der Christus-Erscheinung in der ätherischen Welt*
GA 130   *Esoteric Christianity and the Mission of Christian Rosenkreutz*
GA 131   *From Jesus to Christ*
GA 139   *The Gospel of St Mark*
GA 143   *Erfahrungen des Übersinnlichen, Die drei Wege der Seele zu Christus*
GA 148   *The Fifth Gospel*
GA 157   *Menschenschicksale und Völkerschicksale*
GA 173   *The Karma of Untruthfulness, Volume 1*
GA 179   *Geschichtliche Notwendigkeit und Freiheit Schicksalseinwirkungen aus der Welt der Toten*
GA 199   *Spiritual Science as a Foundation for Social Forms*
GA 224   *Die menschliche Seele in ihrem Zusammenhang mit göttlichgeistigen Individualitäten, Die Verinnerlichung der Jahresfeste*
GA 229   *Das Miterleben des Jahreslaufes in vier kosmischen Imaginationen*

GA 265   *'Freemasonry' and Ritual Work*
GA 268   *Mantrische Sprüche. Seelenübungen Band II, 1903–1925*
GA 292   *Kunstgeschichte als Abbild innerer geistiger Impulse*
GA 293   *Study of Man*

All titles available via Rudolf Steiner Press (UK) or SteinerBooks (USA)

The Lord's Prayer
The Living Word of God
Judith von Halle

'*The contents of this volume have arisen from my own spiritual experience, and do not represent any kind of hypothesis or speculation, except where I expressly say that I am unable to make any definitive statement about a particular event or set of circumstances . . .*'

After she received the stigmata in 2004, Judith von Halle began to experience, very vividly, the events that occurred at the time of Christ. These continuing experiences are not visionary or clairvoyant in nature, but an actual participation, involving all human senses, in the events themselves. To complement this method of witnessing Christ's life, von Halle brings to bear a spiritual-scientific mode of observation—a form of research based on a fully conscious crossing of the spiritual threshold by the human 'I' (or self). Combining the results, she describes in this concise study Christ's presentation of the Lord's Prayer—the archetypal prayer of humanity—to those closest to Him, and the context in which He gave it.

Von Halle considers the historical circumstances at the time of Christ, the preparations He made for passing the Prayer on to others, the Prayer's meaning to the disciples, and how the Prayer itself acts as a mediator between worlds. In addition she reflects on the doxology of the Lord's Prayer, and its relation to the Sephiroth Tree.

96pp; hardback; £9.95; ISBN 978 1902636 85 6